Jean

D1758946

An Illustrated History of
FAREHAM

Jacket illustration : A mid-Victorian oil painting captures the pleasant waterfront scene at Fareham, probably on a regatta day. People are crowding to the riverside while a train passes over the viaduct on its way to Fareham station. What attractions were contained inside the two giant marquees ?

© Copyright Portsmouth City Museum & Art Gallery

An Illustrated History of
FAREHAM

Lesley Burton

and

Brian Musselwhite

ENSIGN PUBLICATIONS

© Copyright Lesley Burton and Brian Musselwhite 1991

All rights reserved. No part of this publication may be reproduced, stored in a retrieval system or transmitted in any form or by any means, electronic mechanical, photocopying, recording or otherwise without the prior permission of Ensign Publications.

The rights of Lesley Burton and Brian Musselwhite to be identified as authors of this work have been asserted by them in accordance with the Copyright, Designs and Patents Act 1988.

First published in 1991 by
Ensign Publications
2 Redcar Street
Southampton SO1 5LL

a division of Hampshire Books Ltd.,
publishers of local books of quality

Publisher : David Graves
Editors : Roy Gasson Associates
Text files : Christine Pacey
Jacket design : Mark Smith
Page make-up : Precinct Press
Repro : MRM, Aylesbury
Printer : Printer Portuguesa, Lisbon

ISBN 185455 040 3

CONTENTS

Towards the end of the eighteenth century, major improvements were made to the main thoroughfares between towns, often under the aegis of the 'turnpike trusts'. Here, near Titchfield, labourers are making repairs to the notoriously atrocious road, hitherto almost impassable in wet weather.

FOREWORD
By Kenneth J. Webb MRTPI, FRSA
Director of Developments, Portsmouth City Council

The histories of the large cities of the south, like Winchester, Southampton, and Portsmouth, have been well recorded over the centuries and information about them is readily available, not only to historians but also to the growing numbers of ordinary people who are interested in learning about the background of the area in which they live. But the histories of some of the smaller towns like Fareham — mostly former market towns — have not been so well recorded, although the interest in their past is as great as in that of the larger towns and cities. In addition, in the last three decades the character of Fareham has changed dramatically, probably more than in the last 2,000 years of its history. The living memories of old Fareham are also rapidly diminishing, so that the publication of this book is not only welcome but timely as well.

My first recollection of Fareham is of visiting the cattle market with my father in the 1930s. Later, in the 1940s, when I was in the army, I remember being driven down West Street in an open-topped Bentley while hitch-hiking home for a weekend's leave. In the 1950s I came with my family, to live in Fareham and have now been a resident for thirty-six years.

Because of my strong family connections in the area, I am told dating back to the 1220s, I am very pleased indeed to be associated with *An Illustrated History of Fareham*. I therefore commend this book to readers as being both of general interest now and a reference for future generations on the interesting and varied heritage of a town in Hampshire.

View of Fareham from Wallington Shore

A rather romantic but attractive engraving of the town in about 1860 made by Newman & Co. of London but published in Fareham by Thomas Mansell. Among the landmarks seen in this view from Wallington are two churches and the railway viaduct, complete with train. Thomas Mansell was not only a publisher but also , intriguingly, a boot & shoe-maker and a malster!

CHAPTER ONE
The Making of Fareham

The past is part of us and nowhere more so than in this piece of southern England, where we are surrounded by the physical evidence of centuries of maritime and military history. Fareham's past is on its doorstep. A good part of it is under our feet, below the surface of the thoroughfares and motorways of the modern town. When the construction workers on the M27 moved in during the 1970s to carve a swathe through the ancient borough of Fareham, their mechanical diggers yielded up many clues as to the activities of our forebears. Axes, flints, pottery, shards, and coins revealed the extent to which successive generations have colonized the land.

Fareham was significantly different from either of its near neighbours, Portsmouth and Gosport. The old Fareham town was at no time confined within walls and ramparts and it had no particular role to play in the defence of Portsmouth Harbour. Its rich agricultural lands and their associated villages could therefore thrive unimpaired by the necessity to build barracks, storehouses, and dockyards. Tucked away in the north west corner of Portsmouth Harbour, sheltered by Portsdown Hill, and favoured with a temperate climate, Fareham's creeks have for centuries provided havens for ships, especially those laying up between the wars with France. On their busy shores there were ships under construction, quays for loading and unloading commodities, and a tidal mill for grinding the corn grown on the slopes of Portsdown Hill. Inland, settlers colonized those Portsdown Hill slopes and formed a predominately rural community. By the 10th century Fareham had its beginnings as a settlement clustered around the ancient church of St. Peter and St. Paul on the safe, rising ground above the Wallington River. From here, the settlers could look out over the quay and creek and get an early sighting of any attack from the sea.

Probably the greatest single influence over the historical development of Fareham was that exercised by the Bishops of Winchester. They held the borough of Fareham from before the time of the Domesday survey, when, we read, its taxes were reduced because of its vulnerability to attack from the Danes. Successive bishops continued to take taxes from the people in exchange for their rights to hold a market, fair, and courts. The bishops were men of enormous wealth and power — at the beginning of the 13th century the see of Winchester was the richest in England, comprising over fifty manors and boroughs across the southern counties. One of them, Peter des Roches, who held office from 1205 until 1238, has given his name to one of the Fareham's finest old houses. Roche Court may have been originally designed as his summer palace. The core of the building is certain mediaeval.

It is really only in the second half of the 20th century that the essentially rural nature of Fareham has been seriously challenged by the growing demands of industry and commerce. Fareham Park, only slightly younger than William the Conqueror's New Forest (made a royal preserve in 1079), flourished for many centuries both as a deer park (subject to frequent poaching) and as a source of timber for the king's ships — its rich woodlands, together with those of Titchfield Park and the Forest of Bere, were the mainstay of the king's shipyards. The park was one of many in the southern counties belonging to the see of Winchester, which owned, in mediaeval times, more deer parks than any other see in England.

The little community of Fareham, sandwiched between its fortified neighbours, Portsmouth and Gosport, did not so much flourish as amble gently through the centuries. Its rich agricultural land was cultivated expertly, establishing Fareham as a marked town of some importance. The town was always overshadowed by its eastern neighbour, Portchester, where since Roman times, a castle had dominated the

upper harbour. The castle had many close associations with
royalty. Queen Elizabeth and many other monarchs slept
there on their way to expeditions to France or sometimes just
for pleasure and relaxation. In 1535 Henry VIII and Anne
Boleyn spent a holiday at the castle, where "they were very
merry and hawked daily". It was Anne's last year of life —
she was beheaded in May 1536. By the end of the 18th
century the castle was being used mainly as a prison and was
somewhat decayed. The Admiralty's Commissioners for the
Sick and Wounded seriously considered using it as a naval
hospital. This would have been an ingenious and cash-saving
solution to the problem of re-using an old or redundant building, a problem by no means unfamiliar to us to-day. In the
event though, the Admiralty went for a "new build" at Haslar,
leaving the castle to French prisoners and English rats.

In 1588, the year of the Armada, the men of Fareham were called to defend their shores against any Spanish
landing. In June, archers and billmen from the villages
around Fareham and from Gosport and Alverstoke were
brought in to the town and stood by, with Fareham men, to
repel any attack. In the event they were not needed — the
Spanish fleet was scattered off the Isle of Wight on 29 July —
but the queen showed her appreciation of the Fareham men
by receiving them in London and thanking them for their
vigilance. There is no record that they were ever paid!

The beginning of the 19th century saw Fareham a
small town of growing importance. Although by now it had
light industries and was a pleasant residential area, its prosper-
ity was still based mainly on agriculture. William Cobbett, the
agricultural labourers' champion and radical reforming journalist, has given us a description of Fareham's fields — on the
south side of Portsdown Hill — at harvest-time in the 1820s :
"It is impossible that there can be, any where, a better corn
country than this. The hill is eight miles long, and about
three-fourths of a mile high, beginning at the road that runs
along at the foot of the hill. On the hill-side the corn land
goes rather better than half way up; and on the sea-side, the
corn land is about the third (it may be half) a mile wide. The

land is excellent. The situation good for manure. The spot the earliest in the whole kingdom."

Standing on the top of Portsdown Hill today it is still possible, at the right time of the farming year and in spite of the intensive development since Cobbett's day, to share his elation at the sight of a vast ocean of waving golden corn.

This period after the long wars with France was a difficult one for rural communities like Fareham. New farm machinery was intruding upon this previously labour-intensive industry. Agricultural labourers were terrified of losing their livelihoods and many of them resorted to desperate measures. Soon local farms echoed to the harsh sounds of rioting and machine-breaking and smoke spiralled above the trees and hedgerows from burning ricks and barns. Cobbett was frequently blamed for this destruction on the farms — on his rides through the southern counties he had used farm workers to rebel against the "cursed engines" and the farmers who were introducing them on their farms.

In the 18th and 19th centuries the coastal villages were often the haunt of smugglers. One man charged with checking the activities of the smugglers in the Fareham area was William Arnold, father of Dr. Thomas Arnold of Rugby School and grandfather of the Victorian poet Matthew Arnold. Appointed Collector of Customs for the Isle of Wight in 1777, William Arnold and his men kept watchful eyes on the villages of Stubbington, Hillhead, Warsash, and Hamble, favoured landing places for contraband goods, mainly liquor and tea. William Arnold died in harness in 1801 and was buried in Whippingham Churchyard, where a memorial attests to his character and skill.

By the mid-19th century local government in England was being reformed and standardized and Fareham, like all other towns up and down the country, felt the changes. In 1849, its motley collection of bailiffs, constables, and an ale-taster was replaced by a Board of Health — Fareham had become one of the new Urban Sanitary Districts with special duties and obligations towards its citizens. A surviving private document from this period gives a unique insight into one aspect of the workings of the Board. It is a contract of 21 April 1866 between the Board and Charles Bastard for watering the streets of Fareham town. Bastard agreed to supply a horse to draw the town's water cart and a man to drive it under the direction of the Surveyor. He was to receive a payment of six shillings "for every day that Horse and Man may work", the work not to exceed ten hours a day.

The ultimate seal on Fareham's stature came in 1894, when it became an Urban District. As the century drew to a close, Fareham became increasingly suburban. Its excellent small shops and its lively market drew in the neighbouring farmers and their families. The building of Forts Fareham and Wallington and later the Naval bases of HMS *Collingwood* and HMS *Daedalus* changed the complexion of Fareham, bringing into the town a different residential mix. In 1932 the old Urban District was enlarged to take in the neighbouring parishes of Crofton, Portchester, Sarisbury, Titchfield, and Warsash.

In 1890 the market town of Fareham had a population of just over 14,000. In 1991, the conurbation of Fareham had a population of almost 100,000 — nearly three quarters that of Portsmouth, its biggest and most famous neighbour to the southeast. This, then, has been the making of modern Fareham. We shall see in the next chapters how the townspeople coped with changes in society and their reaction to both local and national events. Other times had other problems. A hundred years hence historians will be writing much the same sort of thing about us today. In the final analysis, there is always a deep, if paradoxical, sense of relief to discover that the more things change, the more they stay the same!

The cottage at the corner of Portland Street and West Street, where the novelist William Thackeray spent some time as a boy, was demolished in the 1930s to make room for the bus station. Today the memory of this great writer is perpetuated in the Westbury Shopping Precinct by 'Thackeray Mall'.

CHAPTER TWO
Travellers' Tales

The 19th-century novelist William Makepeace Thackeray spent many holidays in Fareham at his great-grandmother's cottage in West Street. Later he was to remember the Fareham of his youth as "a dear little old Hampshire town inhabited by the wives, widows, daughters of navy captains, admirals, lieutenants". Today, the novelist's name is perpetuated in his "dear little old Hampshire town" not by a library, a museum, or even a street but by a thoroughfare — Thackeray Mall — in a thoroughly modern shopping precinct. The pretty cottage where he stayed was pulled down long ago to make way for the bus station. Thackeray's keen sense of humour would probably have been tickled by the link between his name and those two bulwarks of late-19th-century life, commerce and transport.

Thackeray remembered a Fareham where a largely residential West Street contained a pleasing variety of houses and cottages, with the wealthier folk living in Admirals Row at the western end. Many of the fine houses and buildings in High Street that we admire so much today were in his time either brand-new or still to be built. The railway was yet to come, as too were those public buildings that developed with beneficent Victorian urbanization. Thackeray's reference to naval officers and their ladies is echoed in Pigot's Directory of Hampshire for 1830, in which Fareham is described as "eligibly situated on an arm of the sea and chiefly inhabited by persons of maritime occupation". According to Pigot, the population of Fareham at this time was a mere 3,677. Small as it was, however, the Fareham of 1930 was apparently a flourishing place. The directory, mentioning Palmeter's floating dock, used for ship repairs, Burrell's marine stores, the

lively sea-borne trade in coal, corn, and timber, together with
Bartholomew's wrought-iron works at Fontley and the earth-
enware and brick-making industries, suggests a Fareham that
was particularly busy and brisk for all its small size.

Over the years, and in particular the last two centuries, visitors and authors of guide-books to the town have
attempted to describe Fareham, sometimes with insight, often
in great detail. But how local historians wish that it had been
possible for writers of earlier centuries to record their thoughts
and feelings about Fareham! But then, travelling for travelling's sake was a concept unknown to the vast majority of
people in early times — in mediaeval days, few people had the
opportunity to travel away from their birthplace. It would
have been pleasant, too, if the scribes who put together the
Domesday Book had been able to comment more on the nature of the places they visited and assessed; but William the
Conqueror, that practical and pragmatic tyrant, had no interest in things of speculation or imagination. The Domesday
Book presents only the bald facts about "Ferneham" in 1086:
that it was held in demesne by the Bishop of Winchester, that
it consisted of some 3,600 acres (but was assessed on only
two-thirds of this amount in the days of Edward the Confessor,
owing to its need to defend itself from Viking raids), and it had
a church, two mills, and a population of 52.

As the feudal system developed, those early inhabitants of Fareham, tied as they were to work for the lords of the
manors such as the Oyselles at Cams and the Des Roches at
Roche Court in return for the privilege of cultivating a little
area of land for themselves, were at least fortunate in that the
area was fertile. Fareham flourished — its population increased and, partly because the trees in nearby Fareham Park
and Titchfield Park provided timber for shipbuilding, it developed into a place of some importance. Having been granted
the right to become a borough, it was entitled to hold a borough court and an annual fair, and also to send two burgesses
to the parliament of 1306. Sadly, the local worthies of the
14th century soon decided that Fareham could not afford the
costs of parliamentary representation and asked King Edward

III for permission to withdraw from this privilege in 1345. It was to be a long time before the town received such status again!

Something of a decline in Fareham's affairs and trade set in during the next two hundred years. John Leland, antiquary and librarian to Henry VIII, was commissioned by the king to search out manuscripts and relics from the religious houses, monasteries, and cathedrals in England. He toured England in 1535-43 and began to compile from his records a topographical account of the country. In Fareham, apparently, he found little of note. He dismisses the area north of Forton in a few words: "A myle and a half above this is Bedenham Creeke so caullid of a village standing by it. This creek's mouth lyith almost agayn Portechester Castelle. Fareham a fisscher village lyith about a myle more upward at the very hedde of the haven."

But Fareham was far more than a "fisscher village" in the century that followed. A letter from an unknown writer to Sir John Coke, Charles I's Commissioner of the Navy, informed him that "the river leading to Fareham within a mile of the town is an absolute good and safe place to moor ship and in all respects as convenient and safe a harbour as Chatham. £2000 may be saved the king in moorings and men." Advantageous or not, however, Fareham was not destined to become another naval dockyard. Fareham was loyal to King Charles during the Civil War and lost a number of citizens and some livestock in a parliamentary raid in 1645.

Fareham's most important and influential visitor during the next century was John Wesley. That indefatigable and zealous preacher, bravely determined to bring the word of God to the people that he believed the established Church had neglected for so long, travelled the length and breadth of the country preaching in the open air. In 1638 he was in the Isle of Wight, and, having been impressed with his reception in Newport, he recorded in his Journal, "Slipt this humane and loving people and crossed over to Portsmouth. On Sunday I preached in the street at Fareham. Many gave great attention

but seemed neither to feel nor understand anything." But a
few days later he tried again and this time: "A wild multitude
was present yet only a few mocked — the greater part were
soon deeply attentive".

The new ideas in religion which led to the establishment of the Wesleyan Methodist Church throughout the
country were matched by fresh developments in agricultural
methods during the 18th century. The land was used more
effectively, and this, together with increasing specialization and
the more selective breeding of livestock, meant that in 1795
Warner could write in his History of Hampshire: "The soil is
generally rich and the county affords plenty of corn, cattle,
wool, bacon, wood, iron and honey .... the sea coast here
furnishes lobsters, oysters and other sea fish and its rivers
abound in fresh fish, especially trout. The farmers are a
substantial class of men, full of agricultural knowledge and
industry. They are very fond of fine teams of horses, each vies
with his neighbour to outdo him in having better cattle." As to
Fareham itself, Warner found it "a pleasant town, with a
market on Tuesdays and a fair on June 29th. It has a well-
endowed Charity School where children are instructed to read
and write so as to qualify them for useful employment in life.
King Charles dignified this place with the honourary title of an
earldom in creating Madame de Queroval, his mistress, Coun-
tess of Fareham. Cams, south-east of Fareham, is the elegant
seat of the family of Delme".

Warner's "pleasant town" had a population of about
3,000 when he visited it. During the next fifty years the
number of its inhabitants doubled and the process of urbanization that characterized so many little towns in the 19th century was set under way. Almost as if to anticipate the coming
of railways and the development of leisure travel for at least
the reasonably well-off, guide books began to appear more
frequently. At the beginning of Queen Victoria's long reign,
political attention became focused on national consolidation at
home as opposed to foreign adventures. Locally, old and
decrepit buildings on West Street in particular were demolished and replaced by solider structures built with local bricks.

No doubt a visitor to the town in 1836 would have been impressed to see new buildings such as Portland Hall, erected for the Society for Literary and Philosophical Objects to provide both instruction and entertainment for the townspeople. Such an observer would also have welcomed walking along well-kept pavements and roads and would have certainly have remarked favourably upon new gas lamps, an up-to-date amenity provided by the gasworks recently built down by the creek.

Round about the year 1840, two guide-books — Mudie's *Hampshire* and Robson's *Directory of Hampshire* — had plenty to say in praise of Fareham. "Though it is comparatively small there are few towns in Hampshire or indeed in England more pleasantly or more advantageously situated", enthused the contributor to Mudie's book. "It is a great thoroughfare by land and a seaport to a very extensive district. For local trade it is indeed much better situated than Portsmouth itself." Both Mudie's and Robson's books mention Fareham's sheltered situation. "During the summer months it has a large influx of visitors for the benefit of sea-bathing, and a commodious bathing-house has been erected for their accommodation", commented the latter. Robson also referred to the way in which Fareham's local affairs had been conducted for many years: "The government of the town is vested in a bailiff, two constables and two ale-tasters chosen annually by a jury." This somewhat archaic form of local government was shortly to change as a result of the Public Health Act of 1849. From that date Fareham, like many other towns of similar size, was placed under the administration of a local Board of Health which was responsible for the area's well-being. The nine public-spirited members of Fareham's first local board, which was chaired by Richard Porter, were three merchants, three "gentlemen", a brewer, a cooper and basket-maker, and the almost-obligatory naval commander.

Yet another directory of Hampshire, Cravel's, appeared in 1859. Cravel noted that "Fareham is a railway town and has within late years made great advances, for fifty years ago it was merely a village, the houses only cottages;

Trinity Church, West Street, Fareham.

Although the artist's sense of perspective seems to have gone awry — the
lady posting the letter in Fareham's first pillar box appears to be taller
than the coach and horses — this engraving gives us an excellent glimpse
of mid-Victorian Fareham. This time Mansell, the publisher, has managed
to have his name included over the shop but with a 'backward' N — a
result of the engraver having to work in reverse and getting it wrong!

this improvement is chiefly owing to John Barney Esq. who pulled down the old buildings and erected more modern and handsome structures....There is a considerable manufacture of red clay pottery, established by Mr. Thomas Stares of Wallington, nearly the whole of the western counties being supplied. The exports from the town are oak timber, bark, hoops, pottery and bricks."

Indeed Fareham was changing. Two years later, William White's *Hampshire* also refers to the street improvements made during the 1820s and 1830s, but his most interesting snippet of information about the town records one of those fine old skills that was soon to become obsolete with the rapid development of the railways: "Messrs. Cole's coach building factory in West Street (patronised by the Queen and the late William IV) gives employment to about thirty hands and sends carriages to Australia and other parts of the world."

As well as giving a general description of Fareham, White's book also listed most of the residents and their occupations, thus enabling us to build up a fascinating picture of the town at this time. West Street, for example, was obviously no less a varied hive of business then than it is today. As well as Cole's coach-builders, other establishments catered for the needs of horse-drawn transport — in West Street, the main thoroughfare, there were three blacksmiths, Robert Bruce, Thomas Hoare, and Edward Windsor (besides three others elsewhere in the town), a wheelwright, John Dean, and three saddlers, Joseph Hoare, Daniel Pargent, and William Pink. West Street also contained two tailors, four milliners, two chemists, four bakers, two butchers, two cabinet-makers, four watch and clock-makers, two tallow chandlers, two ironmongers, two hairdressers, and as many as six boot and shoemakers. Fresh bread was available from either Jonathan Pannell, Charles Pargent, or George Pink, while James Buckett or Thomas Howard offered their tobacconists' wares for those who indulged in the newly fashionable habit of smoking. Six grocers and four greengrocers are also listed for West Street, but five other shops whose contents presumably defied easy classification are simply listed under "shopkeepers". Also in

A painting by an unknown artist entitled 'The Port of Fareham' depicting the scene from Lower Quay in the days when the town was principally known as a maritime area.

business was Arthur Wyatt, who combined a very old trade with a very new profession as "dyer and photographer".

Two very busy Fareham men of this time were George Boorn and David Harris, who appear in the directory not only as grocers and wine and spirit merchants but also a brick and tile manufacturers. Boorn and Harris were in competition as brick-makers with no less than nine others, including William Cawte at Furze Hall and James Smith at the Old Turnpike, not to mention other earthenware-manufacturers such as George Harris at the Fareham Pottery and the appropriately named Richard Kiln at Wallington.

Compulsory education was still over a decade away in the future, but Fareham already possessed plenty of schools. The directory mentions that "Price's Charity School, in West Street, for the instruction and clothing of 30 poor boys of Fareham Parish, was founded in 1721" and also describes the infant school in Western Lane and the two National Schools in Fontley and Fareham, not forgetting the efforts of William Ashford and Sarah Maine at the depressingly named Workhouse School.

That Fareham at this time was a place of many contrasts is further suggested by the contemporary Ordnance Survey map. What is now the ever-busy main road leading to Gosport then appears to be neither wider nor more important than Newgate Lane or even Windmill Lane. A mid-19th-century traveller approaching Fareham from Gosport would no doubt have admired the fine setting of Fleetlands, the seat of George B. Hall, as he passed. With the new railway line on his left, he would have noticed Earl's Farm, Shambler's Farm, and Blackhouse before skirting the Ropewalk Fields prior to meeting Windmill Lane coming in from the east. He would have been impressed with such attractive houses as Rose Cottage, Southfield House, Elm Villa, and Belvoir as he walked along towards the viaduct by the picturesque waterfront. At this period most of Fareham's residents lived in High Street, West Street, Trinity Street, School Lane, and Charles Street, (Charles Street, named along with Osborn Road after the wealthy local owner of Downend, later lost its name and became simply the south end of Osborn Road.) There were smaller houses in Portland Street and South Street. Fareham's industrial area was at Wallington, where there were potteries, breweries, and tanneries. At Downend, Uplands, and especially Cams the big estates stood proudly as the gentry's bastions against the rise of the common man.

At around this period the town was provided with up-to-date municipal amenities such as a police station (built in 1854 at a cost of only £200 and housing originally a superintendent and three men), a gas works, a market hall, and a fire station. But the towns seems to have settled down into something of a torpor during the latter part of the 19th century. High Street aged quietly and respectably, West Street was gradually filled in with more shops, and houses were built on spare land to serve the ever-increasing population.

In 1881, a new book, *A Tourist's Guide to Hampshire*, sounded a discordant note compared with earlier symphonies of praise for the town. Acknowledging that Fareham's situation was "pretty", it nevertheless complained "there is not much of interest in the town, which is a straggling place about a mile long;...it is, however, a centre of considerable trade...there are two churches, neither of which need detain the tourist". Two decades later, in 1908, a writer in the *Victoria County History of Hampshire* made clear the decline of Fareham as a seaport: "...a few fishermen find occupation round the Cams but the shipping is quite unimportant, the chief article imported being coal." In addition, the writer remarks, "Sheep rearing, once an important industry at Fareham, has died out. A wealthy cattle market is held, but the fair, formerly of great importance, was abolished in 1871." However, agriculture was still doing well, with good corn crops, and brick-making and tanning were still flourishing industries. High Street, with the majority of its houses now over a hundred years old, receives admiration and attention for the first time in a guide-book, while Roche Court is singled out for particular praise.

The development of photography, and particularly the art of capturing a view on a postcard, which came into its own at the beginning of the 20th century, enables us to see exactly what certain parts of the town looked like at this time. Postcards of West Street and High Street show plenty of bustle and vigorous commercial activity, with many of the shops loudly and brightly shouting their wares yet somehow avoiding the garishness of their modern equivalents. On the other hand, postcards of the quay and the mill show them as picturesque retreats for tourists — and how distant now seems the comment in Black's 1913 *Guide to Hampshire* about the quay: "Turning down to the right, beneath the railway, one may find a pleasant walk along this water...."

The tranquil tone was still in evidence in a 1919 guide-book to the area. Fareham was rated "a pleasant little town, the one half of it old-fashioned, the other half modern, and as a whole an ideal residential centre. Ideal as a place in which to acquire a home, because it is neither too large nor too small, because its main street is wide, well-paved and replete with first-class shops, because it has an excellent supply of water, because it has the advantage of electric current available for all purposes, and because — this not the least important factor — Fareham is one of the most conveniently situated and accessible of all Hampshire towns."

Accessible it certainly was. Soon motor-cars and lorries were to make their unwelcome, pollution-laden entry on to the peaceful scene. Between the First and Second World Wars, the shops along West Street developed and diversified as the number of private homes along what came to be known as "Fareham's Golden Mile" diminished. Shop-fronts and the cinemas began to shout their wares with what struck contemporary residents as more jazzy and flashy advertising logos than before, while the first road signs began to add a touch of untidiness. In 1929, Charles Cox in his guide to Hampshire had harsh words for Fareham: "It is a singularly unattractive little town and has hardly any vestige of antiquity pertaining to it. The parish church of St Peter is a strange building. The body of the old fabric was pulled down in 1812 and a huge,

By Particular Desire for O.. Only.

At the Red Lion Assembly R..

Fareham.

On TUESDAY, 7th. Day of MAY, 1816,

WILL BE GIVEN A

CONCERT.

Vocal Performers Mrs. PURVIS, Mr. BEDFORD, and Mr. WEBBER.

RECITATIONS, by Mr. DALTON.

Part First.

		Mrs. PURVIS, Mr. BEDFORD, & Mr. WEBBER
Glee.	"Glorious Apollo,"	
Song.	"Soldier Tir'd"	Mr. PURVIS
Song.	"The Death of Nelson,"	Mr. WEBBER
Song.	"The Sapling,"	Mr. BEDFORD
Duet.	"Take this Nosegay,"	Mrs. PURVIS and Mr. WEBBER
Song.	"Sigh not for Love,"	Mrs. PURVIS
Song.	"When life looks lone and dreary,"	Mr. WEBBER
Song.	"Young Love,"	Mrs. PURVIS
Comic Song.	"What's a Woman like,"	Mr. DALTON
Duet.	"All's well,"	Mr. BEDFORD and Mr WEBBER
Glee.	"Bells of St. Michael's Tower,"	Mrs. PURVIS, Mr. BEDFORD, & Mr WEBBER

RECITATION,

MATRIMONIAL COMFORTS.

Being a Dissertation upon the Conduct of Ladies, and that of their HUSBANDS—The Difference between COURTSHIP and MATRIMONY—A Scene of Matrimonial DISCORD and one of TRANQUILITY—A Receipt for Beauty, with General Observations upon the Marriage State, and how to make Ladies appear Lovely, without the Assistance from Art.

Part Second.

		Mrs. PURVIS, Mr. BEDFORD and Mr. WEBBER
Glee.	"The Wreath,"	Mrs. PURVIS
Song.	"Jessie the Flow'r o'Dumblaine,"	Mr. WEBBER
Song.	"Faithless Emma,"	Mrs. PURVIS and Mr. WEBBER
Duet.	"Together let us range the Fields,"	Mr. BEDFORD
Song.	"The Wreath,"	Mrs. PURVIS and Mr. WEBBER
Duet.	"I Love Thee,"	Mr. WEBBER
Song.	"Death of Abercrombie,"	Mrs. PURVIS
Song.	"Recitative and Polldora,"	Mr. BEDFORD
Song.	"Flow thou regal purple Stream,"	Mrs. PURVIS
Song.	"Oh! Nanny,"	Mr. WEBBER
Song.	"The Temple of Liberty,"	

GRAND FINALE—GOD SAVE THE KING with additional Stanzas on the approaching Nuptials of HER ROYAL HIGHNESS PRINCESS CHARLOTTE OF WALES.

To commence at half-past Seven.—Tickets 3s. each to be had at the Bar of the Red Lion, Fareham.

Mr. LUTMAN, Jun. will preside at the Piano Forte, and Play a Sonata, (Playell) in the first Part, and one with variations in the Second.

Coe, Printer, Fareham

RECITATION
MATRIMONIAL
COMFORTS
*Being a Dissertation
upon the Conduct of
Ladies, and that of
their Husbands
The Difference
between
COURTSHIP and
MATRIMONY
A scene of
Matrimonial
DISCORD
and One of
TRANQUILITY A
Receipt for Beauty,
with General
Observations upon
the Marriage State
and how to make
Ladies appear Lovely,
without the
Assitance from Art.*

A fascinating hand-bill for a concert at the Red Lion Assembly Rooms on May 7, 1816 — 'By Particular Desire for One Night Only' — featuring an interesting assortment of songs, a recitation and a piano sonata. Highlights included 'The Death of Nelson', 'Take This Nosegay', 'What's a Woman like' and 'Death of Abercrombie'. With tickets at three shillings each, only the wealthy could afford the privilege of seeing and hearing Mrs. Purvis and Messrs. Bedford, Webber, Dalton and Lutman. The singing of 'God Save The King' at the end of the evening was something of a departure — additional verses were provided to celebrate the 'approaching nuptials of Her Royal Highness Princess Charlotte of Wales'.

ugly red barn, with interior width of 96 feet in places, was created in its place...." After a brief mention of Holy Trinity church, Cox concludes: "...there are no other buildings of any importance."

Various factors in the 1930s combined to produce problems for Fareham. The population, which had grown only slowly throughout the 1920s, increased by over 50 per cent between 1931 and 1939, partly because of a greater demand for labour in the naval bases. In 1932 Fareham added to its responsibilities the populations of a considerable rural area and the old towns of Portchester and Titchfield. At a time when building materials and labour were cheap, housing estates sprang up at an astonishing rate. After the Second World War the process continued and by 1949 the Max Lock Report commented "Portchester is perhaps the most unfortunate example of vandalism in the whole County. An historic village, with an attractive main street with fine buildings of many different periods, leading to a well-preserved Norman Castle with its keep and curtain wall almost intact, has been swallowed up in a sea of speculative building." Meanwhile, there was little evidence of planning for the future — by 1947 Fareham's population was over 40,000 but its social and leisure amenities and its road system remained barely adequate for half that number of people.

The devastation suffered in this part of Hampshire as a result of the war led to the need for some coherent planning for the area's future. The Max Lock Report, commissioned by Hampshire County Council and Portsmouth City Council, made a very thorough attempt to analyse the needs, prospects, and future development of southeast Hampshire. Of Fareham Lock was critical: "The local development of work and social services has not kept pace with Fareham's growth of population. Local employment is on a small scale, and is mainly in the service industry. Social services such as libraries and community halls are few or are entirely lacking." But he proposed remedies: "The shopping centre on West Street will need room for expansion, and a new road system will help to divert through traffic to the north of the town from its present

49081. CAMS MILL, FAREHAM.

The rear of Cams Mill — much admired, sketched and photographed, but by the time of this photograph much dilapidated as well. Demolished in 1920, it is commemorated with a plaque.

path through the centre. Fareham has proposed to build a
new administrative and cultural centre on a large, vacant site
north of West Street. Provision for commercial and professional accommodation should be made in the West Street
area." The report went on to recommend vast road improvements and to make a plea for sensible planning of future
housing and the provision of social and shopping amenities for
the different neighbourhoods. While warning that a new
sewerage system should be installed as quickly as possible,
Max Lock saw no reason why Fareham should not be able to
"produce a more satisfactory pattern of living for its present
inhabitants as well as for the new. The wide variety of housing existing, and the retention of much of the present centre,
will give the town a great deal of charm and attraction."

The ideas put forward in the Max Lock Report of
1949 were recognisably the origins of the town centre we
know today. But even as they were being realized they were
overtaken. The population increased beyond most expecta-
tions in the 1950s and 1960s, with a particularly big rise of
almost 38 per cent between 1961 and 1971. At the same
time, a newly affluent society found that it could afford cars
and the resultant drop in usage of public transport soon led to
congestion in Fareham's streets. In 1972 an article about
Fareham in *Hampshire Magazine* was headed, "A Town that
Fell Apart". Fareham, said the author, F.C.E. Thurlow, is "a
town without those desirable social amenities, sports and
leisure facilities and public buildings which are essential to the
creation of a satisfactory community." Furthermore, "because
of inadequate provision in public buildings popular ventures
like the Southdowne Musical Society have to use the Portchester Community Centre two miles away....Fareham's Community Centre endeavours to fulfil its purposes in an old barn-like
drill hall." But at last, as the writer concluded, "new con-
structive thinking seems to have emerged from the council
chamber". Soon the decision was taken to alter radically the
centre of the town — a major transformation that has given
Fareham not only a large shopping centre but also a good
public hall, civic offices, a library and a leisure centre, all of
which are well used.

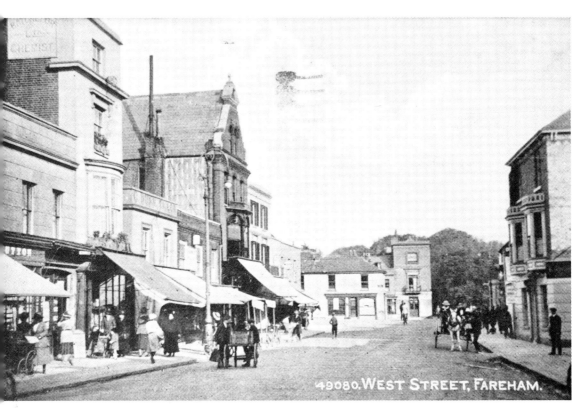

*The eastern end of West Street's 'Golden Mile' of shops in the mid-1920s.
The nearest three shops in the left foreground were long-established
Fareham businesses — Sutton's the stationers and publishers, Batchelor's
the chemist and Dunn's the gentleman's tailor.*

One area that escaped change, of course, was High Street. The architectural historian David Lloyd, who visited Fareham in the 1960s in the course of preparing the Hampshire volume in *The Buildings of England* series, praised High Street, earlier preserved by chance and now by careful control, as one of the finest examples of Georgian and early Victorian architecture in Hampshire. Its buildings remain today, preserved as Fareham's proudest heritage. West Street, however, he found of little distinction, apart from the 1836 Congregational church, the former Corn Exchange with its handsome upper storey, Holy Trinity Church, the railway station, and Westbury Manor. He wrote of the street: "The old facades that remain over the modern shop fronts are mostly of humble former houses, seldom more than two storeys high, and the frequent recent rebuildings have nowhere added positively to the character of the street." "Why", he asked rhetorically, when commercial premises are rebuilt, "cannot a 20th-century character be imparted that is as memorable in its way as the 18th-century character of High Street?" Would he have thought that Fareham's later development of the large shopping precinct and its companion buildings provided the 20th-century character he desired?

How will Fareham look in the year 2000? A recent observer, John Glasspool, in his 1988 book *Solent Shores*, acknowledged that the approach to Fareham by water was most attractive but wrote "Of all the towns around the Solent, this once attractive inland seaport, still graced by fine Georgian buildings, has been most brutalized by road building. The old waterside area has been gutted to make way for roundabouts, overpasses and dual carriageways for commuter links." However, "if you can survive the traffic in one piece, the town's shops are good and varied." Perhaps, one day, someone may be able to devise traffic facilities that are less of an eyesore than they are everywhere at present; but at least during the last twenty-five years the planners have worked hard to correct the lethargy that allowed the town to expand without coherence in the past. Fareham has been described as a shoppers' paradise — let us fervently hope that by 2000 it will not have become a residents' hell.

A far cry indeed fom the fast foods of today. This is the Cedar Cottage in East Street in the 1920s where shoppers, exhausted after a long morning on the 'Golden Mile' could enjoy light lunches or teas in the pleasant interior or on fine days sitting on the circular bench which surrounded the cedar tree itself (far left). The site, now given over to housing, is remembered in name only.

CHAPTER THREE
Lords of the Manor

Lords of the Manor In 18th-century Fareham several influential families presided over their rural acreages like benevolent despots. At Roche Court, on the Wickham Road, the Gardiner family held sway in the mediaeval manor house built by the 13th-century Bishop of Winchester, Peter des Roches. In 1780, Samuel Jellicoe, a former Royal Navy contractor and the business partner of Henry Cort, was moving into his new house, Uplands. He had done well for himself out of the wars with America and — unlike his business partner, Henry Cort, who had been financially ruined — had money to invest in property.

At first a modest dwelling, Uplands was greatly enlarged in the 1840s when John Beardmore bought it from Jellicoe. Beardmore was renowned for his collection of arms and armour and added extra galleries to accommodate the display. In the 1900s much of the collection was auctioned at Christie's and a good deal of it found its way into the British Museum. As a teenager Beardmore had made the Grand Tour of Europe in the company of his aunt, Miss Parke. He recorded his observations on the strange ways of foreigners and of his compatriots in a diary which has been published in the Fareham Past and Present series. The mature Beardmore had financial and sporting interests in shipping and, particularly, in yachting.

Another distinguished local family, the Garniers of Rookesbury Park at Wickham, farmed many acres on the Wickham-London road and, like all these land-owning gentry, provided work and a livelihood for the local villagers. Many of the families married into each other. Frances Garnier became

Place House with 'Stony' or 'Anjou' bridge in the foreground. The latter name explained by the association of Place House with Southwick Priory where Henry VI and Margaret of Anjou were married. It is thought the Royal couple crossed the Meon here on their way to Place House.

the wife of John Delmé in 1791 and partnered her husband in his determination to make Cams Hall the grandest of Fareham's many fine estates.

Of all of these Fareham families, none can match the romance and charisma surrounding the Delmés of Cams Hall. The clue to the origins of the family lies in that acute accent over the final 'e'. The Delmés originated from the province of Lorraine in northern France. They were Walloons of mixed Belgian and French ancestry, the Walloons, like the Huguenots, endured religious persecution in the 16th and 17th centuries. Many of them fled to England, particularly to the wool towns of Southampton and Norwich, and it is at Norwich in 1589 that the first immigrant Delmé, Adrian de le Me, is recorded as holding the office of deacon of the Walloon church. During the next two centuries the family prospered by marrying into the land-owning English aristocracy. One, Pierre Delmé, became a director of the Bank of England and was in 1723 Lord Mayor of London.

The Cams Hall Delmé who concerns us here is Pierre's grandson Peter, born on 19 December 1748. Peter was determined to emulate his grandfather; he was an ambitious young man who developed a taste for art and skill in gaining the friendship of people in high places. In 1769, two months after his twenty-first birthday, he married a noted beauty, Lady Elizabeth Howard, third daughter of the fourth Earl of Carlisle. She became one of the ladies-in-waiting to George III's Queen Charlotte, and through her Peter became acquainted with the Prince Regent. He brought to his marriage the accumulated wealth of his father and grandfather; she brought the political patronage of her father, through whose influence Peter was elected Member of Parliament for Morpeth, which he represented for fifteen years until his death in 1789. The Delmés moved in the highest social circles and it was probably through Lady Betty's brother Frederick, fifth Earl of Carlisle, that Peter made the acquaintance of Sir Joshua Reynolds. The painter was at the height of his fame: Lady Betty at the height of her beauty. These two formidable attributes came together in the painting of his wife and two of

The northern aspect of Cams Hall in the late-1930s. Once the noble seat
of the wealthy Delmé family, this fine residence was built by Jacob Laroux
in 1771.

their children that Peter Delmé commissioned from Reynolds in 1777.

At the time of his marriage Peter Delmé owned various estates, including Earlstoke Park in Wiltshire which he now sold in order to purchase Place House at Titchfield. This had been the home for more than two centuries of the Wriothsley family; it passed eventually, through marriage, to the fifth Duke of Beaufort, from whom Peter acquired it. His path had probably crossed that of the duke during his parliamentary career — like all his fellow MPs he strenuously courted the patronage of the nobility, who in the 18th century had parliamentary seats in their gift. Unfortunately, Lady Betty did not much care for her Titchfield palace — perhaps it was too remote from the London society of which she was an integral part. Within a year or so, Peter Delmé was house-hunting again. He discovered another grand residence, one somewhat easier to reach from London on the new turnpike roads — a distinct advantage to him as an MP. The house, unlike Place House, was virtually new. Cams Hall was the splendidly elegant property of General John Carnac, a senior official of the East India Company. Carnac had engaged the architect Jacob LeRoux to design for him a spacious mansion with a classically pedimented facade and grand south-facing rooms with serene maritime views over the creek from which could be heard the restful sounds of water lapping lazily against the hulls of small boats. To the north the house looked out towards the great sweep of Portsdown Hill. The privacy of the wooded parklands was ideal as a playground for the five small Delmé children. The purchase completed, the family moved in, taking with them many of the fittings from Place House.

Over a period of ten years, the Delmé family system-atically despoiled both the inner and outer fabric of their Titchfield house. Peter Delmé proved himself to be a cultural asset-stripper of the worst kind. He plundered the interior richness of Place House in order to embellish his new Fareham home, a type of Philistinism we are not unfamiliar with today. It is all the more mystifying because Peter Delmé was some-

The south front of Cams Hall, photographed during the 1930s when the mansion was still in private hands.

thing of an art connoisseur and had an eye for beauty. John Delmé was seventeen when his father died; two years later, while still under age, he married Frances Garnier of Rookesbury Park. He continued his father's work of developing and enlarging the estate while tearing down the statuary, fireplaces, and panelling from Place House. It is an unsavoury story — in fact it is one of the ironies of our local history that Place House today is listed as an Ancient Monument under the care and protection of the Department of the Environment while lovely, desolate Cams is a sad ruin.

In the relatively short period that Peter Delmé was lord of the manor, he established his house as a focus of provincial hospitality. The house nestled into a corner of the creek and was enclosed within its plantations, parks, and shrubberies. A gem set in the south Hampshire countryside, it was the perfect place for Peter to bring his jaded parliamentary colleagues, where they could relax and lose themselves. But although Cams Hall was more accessible than Place House, the long and uncomfortable coach journey from London to Cams would have taxed the physical resources of guests. At this period the Fareham - Portchester road was little more than a rough track. Visitors from London probably travelled via the new turnpike roads through to the High Street and thence down to the quay. Once through the gates of the lodge, a brisk gallop down the long drive brought them to their waiting hosts at the Hall's entrance.

Even in its present dilapidated condition, something of Cams Hall's brilliant ambience remains. During the tenure of Peter and John Delmé, England was at a critical moment in its history. From nearby Portsmouth, ships waited on the alert when invasion from France seemed a real possibility and the exploits of Napoleon Bonaparte were the subject of national concern. Visiting Admirals dining at Cams Hall doubtless discussed Lord Nelson's victories over a glass of port. Literary and artistic life was welcomed. May not Sir Joshua Reynolds, portrayer of Lady Betty have called to see his painting in its very attractive setting? Jane Austen and William Makepeace Thackeray, both very familiar with Fareham, would have felt

Below stairs, and in stark contrast to the rest of the house, rather spartan conditions prevailed for Cams Hall retainers. The utilitarian cupboards, table and lights, and the peeling plaster walls are alleviated by the handsome tableware.

at home here. Those social butterflies Mary and Henry Crawford of Mansfield Park would have taken charge of the Cams' entertainments, while the upwardly mobile Becky Sharp would have been in her element.

John Delmé, Peter's heir, died at the early age of thirty-six, but not before he and his wife Frances had produced a formidable tally of eleven children. Ironically, none of his seven sons produced children and his heir John died aged twenty-three. When the seventh son, Seymour Robert Delmé, died in 1894 aged eighty-six, the entire estate went on the market. The auctioneers, King and King, waxed lyrical in their sales catalogue: "Charming situate on the southern slope of the Portsdown range, within six miles of the naval port and garrison town of Portsmouth and Southsea, close to the market and Postal and Telegraph town of Fareham, with its station on the London and South Western Railway (two-and-a-half hours run of London) with Packs of Hounds within easy distance and placed at the north west corner of Portsmouth harbour, by which it is formed into a peninsula. The Lodge [the Hall] gives on to beautifully timbered parks, gently undulating towards the south, thereby securing charming views over Portsmouth Harbour, the Solent and the Isle of Wight."

The catalogue goes into great detail about the rooms and their fittings, many of which had been torn from Place House. The house had over thirty rooms and an additional suite for the servants. A huge conservatory with tiled floors and an ornamental fountain looked out over the south-facing lawns. There were farms, orchards, a rookery, a wilderness with shaded walks, three vineries, the North and South parks, and Home Farm itself, with stabling and coach-houses. The sale, when it was eventually made, proved a huge disappointment to the family. On Saturday 4 May, 1895, *The Standard* newspaper reported: "The Cams Hall Estate at Fareham, Hants, was unsuccessfully offered for sale last year by Messrs. King and King of Portsea. Since then the East Cams Farm portion has been disposed of and on Tuesday last the home portion was put up for sale. It comprises the mansion, with grounds and parks and agricultural land, 256 acres in all, and

The nursery at Cams Hall in 1936. Most notable, in this almost
archetypal nursery for a privileged child of that period, is the fine rocking
horse, the Landseer print and an attractive Noah's Ark frieze. One
wonders what other period childhood treasures are hidden from view in
the large wardrobe.

the Manor of Cams Oysell. The estate realised £10,250.

By one of those strange ironies peculiar to the Cams Hall saga, the 1777 Reynolds portrait of Lady Betty Delmé and her children was auctioned at Christie's on 7 July 1894 and fetched the then unprecedented sum of £11,000, exactly £750 more than the entire Cams Hall estate. The new owner of Cams Hall was Montague Foster of Stubbington House School and from that moment the house began its slow decline. The Foster family sold off parts of the estate and successive owners this century have tried and failed to cope with the expense of maintaining the property and grounds without the cheap local labour available in Victorian times.

It seemed at one point that even the Royal Navy had it in for Cams Hall! It appeared that gunnery practice on Whale Island by the sailors of HMS *Excellent* had disturbed the peace and the safety of Cams Hall when shot had landed on the lawns close to the house. In order to reinforce these baseless claims, a party of sailors set off from Whale Island in a small boat with a 32-pounder shot on board. Under cover of darkness they landed at Cams, dug a scattered-looking furrow in the lawn close to the drawing room, placed the shot in the prepared furrow, and retreated stealthily to their boat in the creek. The morning light revealed the shot on the grass and a horrified housekeeper complained to the commander-in-chief of HMS *Excellent*, who asked for a full explanation of the practical joke.

At the beginning of the Second World War the house was requisitioned for use by the Admiralty. It has remained empty and derelict since 1945, when the Admiralty staff left it to return to the Dockyard. It was again auctioned in 1948 for a sum of £33,900. Fareham Urban District Council were keen to purchase it in 1954, but at that time no government loan was available. However, Hampshire County Council bought part of the grounds to develop the Fareham Grammar School for Girls. Other parts of the estate were given over to caravanning and agricultural use. In 1977 the council granted outline planning permission for the partial demolition of the, by now, rapidly deteriorating house. The developers wanted to retain the Adam brothers' north facade and construct behind it a modern office block and to make the Home Farm buildings into a leisure centre with a golf course, picnic areas, a children's farm, and an adventure-play area. The plan was an ambitious one, sounded attractive on paper, and would have covered the 230 or so acres with a variety of leisure activities at a cost of approximately £1m. It had Fareham Council's approval but was opposed by the Portchester Society, which objected to yet another golf course. Other objections came from the caravan-dwellers, who were anxious as to their fate should the scheme go ahead. The Ministry of Agriculture finally put paid to the scheme in 1978 by objecting to the Cams Grade 2 agricultural land being used for leisure purposes. The next ten years degenerated into a kind of black planning farce as application succeeded application and was met with objections and counter-objections.

In October 1981 a severe fire threatened what now remained of Cams Hall, spread to the woodlands, and put the caravanners at risk. The architectural practice of Hedley Greentree approached Fareham Council in 1982 with a plan for a large-scale business park, with Cams Hall as its centre-piece, and a golf course. The £6m scheme would have created 600 jobs. The council disapproved — one councillor feared that the business park would be so big that it would turn out to be a "mini-I.B.M." — and the scheme was thrown out. The council then, at this rather late stage in the proceedings, recommended that the whole Cams estate should be declared a Conservation Area, with improvements to the now rather tattered site landscape.

In 1983, the Hedley Greentree practice put forward a scaled-down version of their business-park scheme, which they hoped would be more acceptable to the council and indeed it appeared that, despite protests from the caravanners and nearby residents, the scheme would go ahead. In 1985 it was announced that bats had been found in the Cams ruins, making consultation with wildlife experts an imperative. In the same year a public enquiry decided in favour of the scaled-down plan. This time it was Hampshire County Council's turn to object, on the grounds that the scheme could constitute a departure from the Fareham Review Town Map of 1968, in that part of the site had been designated Public Open Space, and that even in its scaled-down form it represented a "gross" overdevelopment of a sensitive site.

There have since been further applications — one scheme was to turn the Hall into an hotel and flats (which would at least have allowed public access to the restored building) and another was for 200 houses in a "village" setting. In 1988 the site was purchased by Charles Church, a Surrey firm of builders, who immediately set about shoring up the crumbling building with the help of a firm of specialist contractors and the approval of the Hampshire Buildings Preservation Trust. Tragically, a building worker was electrocuted in the process of putting up scaffolding. The dispute about the site goes on while Cams Hall awaits the healing hands of a developer who can satisfy the differing aspirations of Hampshire County Council, Fareham Borough Council, and the people of Fareham.

The process of tanning leather was highly skilled and Wallington tannery was famous for its high quality products. Here the 'fleshers', whose unpleasant job it was to scrape the fat and tissue from the hides, pause with their be-suited overseer to pose for this turn of the century photograph.

CHAPTER FOUR
Working Fareham

The Leathermen
of Wallington

The urban village of Wallington is today one of Fareham's Conservation Areas. It is a desirable residential area on Fareham's eastern flank and, but for the motorway arching over it, has the air of a peaceful backwater. But it was once an important settlement — it was probably the Saxons who secured the high ground overlooking the ford over the River Wallington, where the church of St. Peter and St. Paul now stands. This 13th-century church later served as a good look-out post over Fareham Creek.

But Wallington's foremost historical claim to fame lies in its early industries, which were crucial to the local economy and which provided work for generations of Fareham men. Perhaps the most important industry was tanning. The Rolfe family of Wiltshire started a tannery at Wallington in the reign of Charles I. By the end of the 17th century William Rolfe had built up a thriving and profitable family business, which was strengthened when his daughter Jane married Peter Thresher, another native of Wiltshire. Both men became involved in the community life of Fareham. Rolfe served a term as churchwarden and the Threshers figured prominently in the Fareham "establishment", becoming magistrates, churchwardens, and clergymen. The last owners of the tannery were the Sharlands from Devon. Like their predecessors, the Sharlands, who settled in one of Fareham's handsome old houses in the Broadcut and later moved to the High Street, were very active in the community.

The site of the Wallington tannery, close to the River Wallington and near the busy little commercial port at Town Quay, was an ideal one — hides ready for distribution could be easily shipped to all parts of the British Isles. Business prospered even more in the 1840s when the railway arrived in Fareham, bringing the important and lucrative leather markets within a few hours reach. In a plastic age, it is perhaps all too easy to underestimate the importance of high-quality leather to a less sophisticated society. Apart from its use for everyday items of clothing such as boots, shoes, gloves and hats, leather was essential to the whole world of transport. Coaches and waggons were composed largely of wood and leather, while the ubiquitous horse needed to be saddled and bridled. The army and the navy, too, used leather in quantity and Portsmouth at the time was dominated by the army and navy and by their barracks and shore establishments. There was no tannery in Portsmouth and the Wallington tannery was ideally placed to supply the Victorian armed services with leather for their horses, uniforms, and battle needs.

The process of tanning is at least seven thousand years old and among skilled early practitioners were the Hebrews. The system practised all those centuries ago had scarcely altered in its essentials and was employed at the Wallington works for over three centuries. The men arriving at the tannery started their working day by collecting oak bark from Fareham railway station where it was loaded into horse-drawn carts and transported to Wallington. Here the crushed bark, mixed with Valencia nut, was put in tan or liquor pits, vats made of plank boxes sunk into the ground. Meanwhile hides were arriving at the railway station from all parts of the country. At the tannery, men prepared each skin by removing the rump and tail and the "burr" — unwanted but edible pieces which became the workers perks. Next, men known as "fleshers" scraped the fat and tissue from the hides, which had previously been steeped in lime pits to facilitate the removal of the hair and fat. The lime-soaked hides had many rinsings before they began the first of the immersions in the tan pits. This process could take up to eighteen months as each skin progressed to stronger solutions in the several pits. Lastly came the drying and rolling operation, a very skilled business designed to ensure a smooth, scratch-free leather. At this final stage, any blemish, however slight, could seriously lower the value of the leather.

Leather-making then was a demonstrably long-winded process. Leather workers tended to keep the skills in the family and generations of Fareham fathers, sons, and grandsons followed each other in this very local industry. Wallington tannery was famous for very fine quality leather and its reputation nationwide was high. It had readily available natural assets. Water from the River Wallington was pure and swiftly flowing, abundant supplies of bark were close at hand from the New Forest and the Forest of Bere, and, before the coming of the railway, Fareham Creek was the embarkation point for the export of the leather.

Nothing was wasted at the tannery. The drained bark was dried in the sun by the banks of the river and made excellent fuel for cottage fires or for smoking hams from pigs reared in Wallington backyards. As the family interest in the tannery faded, the business went into a slow decline. It finally closed just before the First World War and remains now only as a memory in the minds of older residents.

The Brick & Tile Industries of Fareham

Fareham's former industrial fame came from its reputation for manufacturing fine quality bricks, tiles, and pots. The industry flourished over many centuries but was at its peak in the 18th and 19th centuries, when Fareham made a great variety of clay products — bricks and tiles, chimney-pots, drain-pipes, and all kinds of pots for domestic and industrial use. Little evidence of this once-flourishing industry exists today, except in some street names, such as Redlands Lane or Kiln Road.

The first brickmakers here were the Romans. To make their bricks, early Roman builders used dried and crushed seashells mixed with mud from the creeks to form a stiff paste. But although shellfish, particularly oysters, were prolific in and around Portsmouth harbour — and were a staple part of the Roman diet — they were not plentiful enough to form the basis of an extensive manufacturing industry. So it was the discovery of the underlying rich clays

During the 1920s, the Fontley brickyards had to meet competition from imported bricks from Belgium. To counteract this the Fontley yard produced millions of tiles for the world market. Here tiles are being unloaded from the firm's bogie on its own siding on to the mainline just north of the Fareham tunnels. The works siding finally closed in 1962.
By kind permission of Fred Hoare

in the area that, in a very literal sense, formed the foundation of the Fareham brick and tile industry.

By the 18th century brick and tile works abounded in Fareham. The vast majority of these were very small and most of them were owned and operated by local farmers who were in effect exploiting the land beneath their farming activities. The two largest concerns were the Bursledon and the Fontley works. The brickyard at Fontley, which stood opposite the abattoir, took its clays from Fontley Copse. The clay had to be made up with loam to achieve the required firmness, otherwise it was subject to shrinkage during firing. The resulting brick was known as the "London Blue". Local village boys starting as young as fourteen years of age, worked in the yards and many stayed for the whole of their working lives. For the male population of Fontley, if you didn't work at the brick and tile works you didn't work anywhere.

In the first half of the 19th century the brickmaking industry received a major boost with the development of the railways. The need to build tunnels to take the railways through Portsdown Hill led to a huge increase in local brick production, particularly in the Fareham yards. So too did the new railways' demands for bridges, culverts, and viaducts — the great Quay viaduct is the Fareham brick industry's most impressive and enduring testimony. Just a few years later, in 1859, British foreign policy under Palmerston gave a further impetus to the local brickmakers. The construction of the line of forts around Portsmouth and Plymouth known colloquially as "Palmerston's Follies" ensured full employment and big profits for local yards.

Mass production of bricks became possible after 1850 with the introduction of new machinery, but at Fontley the handmade tradition continued at least until the mid-1920s, when the import of bricks from Belgium put the Fareham yards in direct competition with European suppliers. This was offset to a considerable extent by the export of millions of tiles from Fontley.

The bricks known as "Fareham Reds" were undoubt-
edly the jewels in the crown of the Fareham industry. From
the early 18th century on, it has been said, they "brightened
the face of London", where they were used in the construction
of the Royal Albert Hall and of St Thomas's Hospital, opened
in 1871 by Queen Victoria. Nearer home, Gosport's Grange
Aerodrome was built with Fareham Reds, as was Osborne
House on the Isle of Wight. And across the world the burgh-
ers of Cape Town chose the Reds to build their town hall.

Handsome blue-grey Fareham brick much used in the
18th century was produced by a burning process. These
bricks can be seen in many fine town houses in the area,
particularly in High Street.

Fareham and Wickham have always enjoyed a reputation for an impressive collection of handsome Georgian and
Victorian buildings and this is owing largely to the high quality of the local brickwork. As Fareham grew in importance
from a thriving 18th-century commercial port to a favoured
residential area for naval officers and their families, the brick
and tile workers rose to the occasion. Fine houses required
quality clayware for drainage pipes, garden pots, jars for
storage, and, of course, chimney-pots. The name of Thomas
Stares figures prominently in this interesting and substantial
subsidiary to the brickmaking industry. In the early years of
Queen Victoria's reign, Stares advertised his red-clay pottery
products, including draining bricks and tunnel cylinders for
water conduits. A directory for Hampshire dated 1857 tells
that these were supplied "to nearly all the Western counties".

The best known of these subsidiary products are the
Fareham "pots", the affectionate nickname for the distinctive
handmade chimney-pots forever associated with 19th-century
Fareham. Typically, the cylindrical pots are about 4ft in
height and taper from a diameter of about 12" at the base to
about 9" at the top. They have a half-round rim at top and
bottom. There is sometimes a piecrust extrusion and then
below that one or more bands of white slip, some of a wavy or
geometric design. The pots had to be made in two parts —

they were so tall that it was impossible for the average-sized potter to reach the whole way down into the pot. The two halves had to be joined together before firing, and while still damp, with slip from the same clay. The two halves were rarely of the same thickness and because of the low-firing clay, distortions occurred. This gave the finished pots an attractive, non-standard appearance much prized by collectors. Possibly the most famous potteries were at North Hill and these continued to produce chimney-pots until the late 1950s. After the Second World War the business changed in character and moved over to Denmead, where its products may be encountered today on the shelves of local department stores.

The one living link with this old Fareham industry was broken by the death a few years ago of Charlie Carver, who had spent all his working life at the potters' cottages at North Hill. It was his hands that appeared in the famous Interlude of the potter's wheel on early BBC television.

The Pipes of Portchester   The earliest English clay pipes date from the first quarter of the 17th century, but it was not until tobacco became comparatively cheap, by the middle of the same century, that clay-pipe smoking became at all widespread. Because the pipes were so easily broken, natural wastage was high, and demand soon became enormous. As a result, by the end of the 17th century there were large numbers of clay-pipe makers in England and the price dropped to a figure within almost everybody's reach.

Portchester was a latecomer to the industry. Clay-pipe manufacture seems to have started there at the end of the Napoleonic Wars. It continued for almost a hundred years and made a small but significant contribution to the economies of Fareham and Gosport. Throughout the period the industry was dominated by two local families, the Russells and the Leighs.

Portchester clay was unsuitable for pipe making and, in the early years of the industry, the china clay used came from Alum Bay in the Isle of Wight. By 1820, though, the

A skilled craftsman at one of the Portchester works making a clay pipe. During the heyday of the industry, between 1890 and 1910 over 7,000 pipes were made every week. Many of these were exported, with France being a major market.

superiority of china clays from the West Country over those from the Isle of Wight was acknowledged. The clay arrived at a wharf close to Paulsgrove, was loaded on to carts, and driven to Portchester.

The production process was a simple one. First the clay was improved and whitened by adding to it chalk from the nearby Paulsgrove Quarry. (No trace now exists of this quarry, which was destroyed to make way for the M27 motorway.) The china and chalk mixture was crushed manually to a fine powder and water added to it to turn in into a paste that could be kneaded like dough. Roughly shaped, it was put into the bottom half of the pipe mould. The top half of the mould was positioned over it and the complete mould put into a vice. A wire needle kept the stem hollow and a plunger over the vice hollowed out the bowl. The mould was then taken from the vice and the wire drawn from the stem. The pipe was removed from the mould and the bowl carefully trimmed into shape. After drying, the pipe was placed in a fireclay dish known as a "sagger", which went into the kiln to be fired. Finally the bowl was decorated and the mouthpiece painted to prevent it sticking to the smoker's lips.

The finished products were packed at sixteen to the dozen. This was to allow for breakages in transit, the long slender stems being very fragile. Broken pipes were sold cut-price to the poor and to gypsies. The pipes were decorated in a variety of styles, dictated by the fashions of the day or the special tastes of buyers. In the mid-Victorian period there was a demand for pipes bearing the crests or badges of regiments or ships. The old wooden hulk HMS *St. Vincent* was at one time moored in Fareham Creek and examples of its attractively decorated pipe bowls have been recovered from the bed of the creek.

All classes of men and some women, particularly gypsies, smoked these pipes, which were despatched from Portchester to many markets, particularly London. Seamen traditionally enjoyed smoking clay pipes and sailors from men-of-war sheltering in Portsmouth Harbour must have been

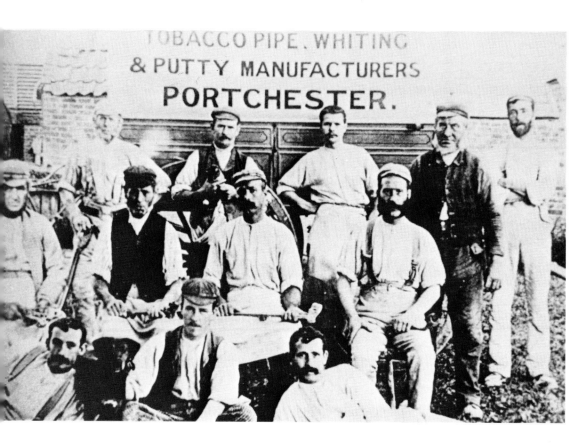

The workmen of Leigh's Tobacco Pipe, Whiting & Putty Manufacturers of Portchester pose proudly for a late-Victorian photographer

among the customers for this local product. The rich mud of the harbour has frequently yielded up specimens of locally made clay pipes, thrown or dropped overboard, and there are good examples in several local museums. The heyday of the pipe-making industry was between 1890 and 1910.

During this period over 7,000 pipes a week were made and despatched to all parts of the United Kingdom and to France — French fishermen enjoyed smoking the long-stemmed variety and these pipes started out on their cross-Channel journey on barges sailing from Fareham Quay.

There were some small pipe-making works outside Portchester. In the late Victorian period, the Goodall family were making clay pipes at Gosport in North Cross Street and there were other works at the Old Turnpike, Fareham, and at St. George's Square, Portsea.

As with so many aspects of economic life, changing fashions dictated slow decline in the popularity of claypipe smoking. First the cigar and then the cigarette began to take over from the pipe and, from the middle of the 19th century, for pipe smokers, briar began to displace clay. By the end of the First World War production at the Portchester works had declined dramatically. In its final years only special and commemorative pipes were being made.

Buy My Sweet Strawberries!

In the period following the Napoleonic Wars when the radical journalist William Cobbett was engaged in his marathon progress on horseback through the southern counties, he made some memorable observations. "From Fareham to Titchfield village a large part of the ground is a common enclosed some years ago", he wrote in *Rural Rides*. "It is therefore amongst the worst of the land in the country." The bulk of the better-quality land was soon taken up by shrewd local farmers with an eye for a bargain and many market-gardening enterprises were started at this period. There still remained, however, large acreages capable of exploitation.

No satisfactory explanation has yet been offered to

During the strawberry picking season as many as twenty 'strawberry specials' a day were loaded at Swanwick station. This pre-First World War photograph shows growers, carters and packers pausing during the protracted business of loading one of these (L.S.W.R.) trains. Young children with time-off from school were employed at threepence an hour to work in the confined space of the tightly packed goods wagons.

By kind permission of F. Emery-Wallis.

account for the remarkable development of the strawberry-growing industry that was to flourish for more than a century and which was to have an extremely favourable impact upon the market economy of Fareham and its surrounding villages. It has been suggested that the very first strawberry plants to be commercially cultivated had been stolen from the lands of one or other of the great houses of Fareham and its environs. This seems entirely feasible. Seasonal labour would have been brought in to harvest the produce from the large acreages of Rookesbury Park, Sarisbury Park, or Cams Hall. The entire estate of Cams Hall, for example, extended over 300 acres. We know that it was solely in the grounds of these large houses in the 18th and early 19th centuries that soft fruits were grown for the delectation of the upper classes. The traditional mildness of the south Hampshire climate helped to produce the occasional out-of-season treat. For example, on 7 December, 1818, *The Hampshire Telegraph* reported: "On the first of this month was gathered from the garden of H.P. Delmé, Cams Hall, a large plate of strawberries in high perfection — a circumstance never before remembered by the venerable gardener who has resided on the premises more than half a century." Whatever the method of introduction, by the early Victorian period the strawberry industry was well established and Titchfield Common had been transformed.

The southerly aspect of the Common, with the Isle of Wight giving protection from the elements, invariably produced a bumper harvest. It was a highly labour-intensive process and provided work for both young and old. Such was the productivity of these growing fields that it was estimated that between two and four acres of strawberries was sufficient to support a family throughout the year. The commercial success of the soft-fruit business generally received a further boost by the break-up of many of the large estates in Fareham and the surrounding villages. Servicemen returning from the First World War were able to buy small plots of land through subsidies made available by the government and the County Council.

The strawberry industry perhaps more than most,

Swanwick railway station with at least one of the sidings occupied with strawberry loading and with more well-laden carts arriving by the minute. Originally this activity went on at Fareham itself but with Swanwick opening in 1887 most of the traffic found that a more convenient rail-head. Botley, too, handled a vast amount of strawberry traffic.

benefitted from the coming of the railways. Much of the produce prior to 1845 was sold to the comparatively local markets of Fareham, Portsmouth, and Southampton, within easy distance by horse-drawn wagon for such a highly perishable fruit. The railways brought the strawberry fields within reach of London and even of Scottish markets. Initially, Fareham railway station was the loading point, until Swanwick station was opened in 1887. In 1913 over 3,000 tons of strawberries were loaded at Swanwick and in the season up to twenty "strawberry specials" left the little station every day.

Every year, from the middle of May onwards, the strawberry-pickers descended upon the fields. Their exuberance and vitality is still remembered by some older inhabitants and legends have grown around them as they have around the hop-pickers of Kent. Gypsies in brightly painted caravans and other itinerant labourers converged in their hundreds on the lanes leading to the strawberry fields to reinforce the local village workforce. The pickers were known locally as the "Joe pickers", after the best-known variety of strawberry, the Sir Joseph Paxton. The neighbouring gentry organized tea and games and this motley flock's spiritual welfare was in the care of the Church Army. God was asked to bless their labours but He seems to have had little control over their evening activities. Saturday-night fights outside the pubs in Swanwick were frequent and highly vocal. Children watched from bedroom windows as men fought in the streets below and women egged them on.

Nothing was allowed to interfere with the strawberry harvest. It is on record that village celebrations for the coronations of both Edward VII and George V were postponed until such time as the ripe berries were safely gathered in. Even at this comparatively late period local schoolchildren were still a vital part of the labour force and school managers would arrange early summer holidays to coincide with the ripening of the fruit. These were known as "strawberry holidays" — later holidays were "blackberry holidays". There were two interesting off-shoots to the strawberry industry. In the earlier period when the bulk of the transport was by horse-drawn

Stawberry specials call no more at Swanwick station and the network is the poorer for that, but some of the atmosphere of those days can still be found there today. This 1970s photograph shows off the canopied shelters and the pleasant view down the line.

wagon the resultant abundant supplies of manure was used to enrich the shallow and stony soil of the strawberry fields. A basket-manufacturing factory was established at Sarisbury, where the long slender trunks of imported poplars were converted into thin strips and then woven into the large, flat baskets in which the strawberries were conveyed via wagon and train to their outlying destinations, there to arrive in pristine condition within a few hours. Nothing was ever wasted during the making of these baskets. The round inner logs remaining after the shaving process were sold off to villagers for firewood.

At the turn of the century, the strawberry growers, pickers, and wagoners formed the Swanwick Fruit Growers' Association, which put the whole industry on a more commercially cohesive basis. The Association was able to use its united strength to negotiate better terms with the railway companies and to fix prices at the big markets. It also learned to cope with such problems as adequate supplies of water to the fields. Until 1908 there was no piped water to either Swanwick or Sarisbury. Water had always been imported to the strawberry crop. Too little means small berries, too much turns them mouldy.

The success of the Fruit Growers' Association was soon established. In 1928, for instance, records show that a stupendous total of 1,287,925 baskets left Swanwick Station that summer for the highly lucrative markets in London and the provinces. These figures were a clear vindication of the effectiveness of marketing the strawberry harvest by speaking with a unified voice. In the early years of this century over 2,500 acres annually were given over to the cultivation of strawberries in Hampshire. The bulk of this rich harvest was centred around Fareham. By 1968 the acreage had been reduced to less than 600, but the output was still impressive. The heyday of the Fareham strawberry industry has long since departed. The strawberry fields of Titchfield, Locks Heath, and Sarisbury have had to compete in recent times with the ever-rising demand for land for housing and light industry. Only old photographs, of pickers standing amid their piled-high baskets, of the attendant waggons with their thick-maned heavy horses, remain to convey something of the flavour of a colourful and productive chapter in Fareham's rural history.

William Cobbett describes a visit he made "to the house of farmer Mears" at Durley near the village of Botley in the 1820s. He notes that "Mrs Mears, the farmer's wife, had made, of the crested dog's tail grass, a bonnet which she wears herself" and goes on: "I there saw girls platting the straw. They had made plat of several degrees of fineness; and, they sell it some person or persons at Fareham, who, I suppose, make it into bonnets." Cobbett's name is not the first that would spring to mind in any discussion of the history of fashion, but he clearly foresaw the possibilities of a thriving cottage industry for the wives and children of the rural labourers whose cause he championed. He points out that each of the girls he saw plaiting straw at Durley "earns per week as much (within a shilling) as her father, who is a labouring man, earns per week". Women and children from the Portsdown villages gathered the dried grasses as well as the straw left over from the harvest. These were made up into plaits and sold to milliners in Fareham who made them up into fashionable bonnets. Both the plaits and the hats made from them were later known as "leghorns", after the Italian town in which they originated.

Numbers of very young children were employed in the business, their small, nimble fingers being capable of producing plaits of the finest texture. It was often a hazardous and unpleasant occupation because the straw and dried grasses cut and grazed the skin. The plaiters would pass the strands between their lips to flatten and moisten the finished product and this action cut the lips and tongues of the young plaiters.

The Fareham straw-plaiting industry gave much-needed employment to the families of poor labouring women in the post-Napoleonic period. Very little research has been done on this interesting aspect of Fareham's cottage industries. It seems likely that Mrs Mears of Durley became the guiding light of the Fareham workers, for we read in *The Hampshire Chronicle* for May 1824 that the Society for Arts awarded her a silver medal and £5 for a bonnet made under her supervision from a grass plait. The straw-plaiting business died out in the middle of the 19th century, its demises hastened by the decline in demand from the fashion industry and the competition of cheaper imports from the Continent.

Fareham's
Salterns

In these days of mass refrigeration and freeze drying, it is easy to underestimate the problems our ancestors must have faced in trying to keep their food fresh and edible, particularly meat and fish. One method they had of preserving these foods was by rubbing them with salt or immersing them in a brine solution. The age-old industry of salt-gathering was once very common around our coasts, usually in estuaries or creeks where areas of flat marshland could accommodate the large shallow pans in which the sea water was collected. The process of reducing the volume of water by evaporation until it was ready for boiling was a lengthy one. Perhaps the best eye-witness description of the working of the salterns as they were called, comes from the pen of Celia Fiennes, an enterprising gentlewoman with strong Hampshire connections. Between 1682 and 1702 she made numerous journeys on horseback around the country making observations on the manners, customs, and industries of the time. She watched with deep interest the salt-workers of Lymington going about their business. She wrote: "The sea water they draw into trenches and so into several ponds that are secured in the bottom to retain it and it stands for the Sun to exhale the watry fresh part of it and if it prove a dry summer they make the Best and most salt for the rain spoyles the ponds by weakening the Salt: when they think its fit to Boyle they draw off the water from the ponds by pipes which conveys into a house full of large square iron and copper panns, they are shallow but they are a yard or two if not more square, these are fixt in rowes one by another, it may be twenty on a side in a house under which is the furnace that burns fiercely to keep these panns boyling apace, and as it candy's apace about the edges or bottom so they shovel it up and fill it in great Baskets and so the thinner part runs through the moulds they set to catch it which they call Salt Cakes; the rest in the Baskets drye and is very good salt.."

It does not require much effort of imagination to relocate this busy scene to the shores of Fareham Creek. There are plenty of clues on the map to help us locate the sites where the saltmakers pursued their ancient trade. Salterns Lane, winding off from the eastern side of the A32 road to Gosport leads down to the former Salterns Quay. In the southeast corner of the creek are the former Cams saltmarshes. At Hillhead, the name Salt Lane is another clear indication of the existence of saltworks in past centuries. To judge from the Domesday records, the most valuable of the many saltings in the Fareham area was that of Boarhunt Manor, which centuries ago extended as far as the shores of Cams Bay.

The early saltworkers left few clues as to the uses, other than domestic, to which their produce was put. But the navy required vast quantities of salt for the pork, beef, and mutton supplied to ships of the line. This requirement continued until well into the 19th century, until canning processes were perfected. The Admiralty had a large victualling department at Portsmouth which was later, in the early 1800s, transferred to Gosport. It is not unreasonable to suppose that in earlier centuries the enterprising saltmen of Fareham might have sold the produce of their salterns to the Admiralty's victualling departments in Portsmouth harbour.

Fareham's salt industry died out more than a century ago. It had always been subjected to punitive taxes by successive governments. The salt tax began to bite into the saltmens' profits during William III's reign (1689-1702) and by the time of the Napoleonic Wars it had risen to 15 shillings a bushel. Another important factor in the decline of the industry was the cost of carting the huge amounts of coal needed for the boiling process. All that remains today of this very ancient craft are those evocative place-names on our local maps.

Henry Cort and the English Iron Industry

Arguably, the most distinguished person to be associated with Fareham's industrial past, Henry Cort was an essentially simple man whose ideas were exploited by others more cynical and worldly wise than himself. Cort was born in Lancaster in the year 1740. We know very little about the young Cort and his early years, except that he was the son of a builder and brickmaker, perhaps rather an appropriate background for the future Fareham industrialist.

Cort's first recorded profession is that of navy agent in the year 1765, when he was twenty-five years old. Prior to his marriage in 1768 to Elizabeth Heysham he was living in Crutched Friars in the City of London. There has been speculation as to how Cort became involved in the business of iron manufacturing. One possible explanation suggests itself. His wife was the niece of one Mr Attwick, who held a lucrative contract to supply the dockyard with mooring chains and assorted naval stores made of iron. In 1772, however, Attwick sold his contract to Thomas Morgan, a Gosport smith. At some time during the next three years Cort took over Morgan's contract and with it his working premises at Gosport. This site was known as The Green; it stood at the south side of what is now the lower end of Mumby Road. From 1775 to 1784 Henry Cort worked in his forge on The Green, supplying the dockyard with its day-to-day requirements for iron goods and equipment. Cort's close business relationship with Navy Board officials and his dealings with Navy Board staff at the nearby dockyard in Portsmouth impressed upon him the immense importance of good-quality wrought iron. Cort was an innovator as well as a contractor, and in about the year 1779 he took over a forge at Fontley, where he began a five-year-long experiment with an iron puddling process. There is reason to believe that at least one other forge was operational at Fontley well before this period. The area was, and remains, largely rural, with rich supplies of timber for the forge and the River Meon supplying the power to work the great tilt hammer.

Cort, then, was operating on two sites and investing large sums of money into his enterprise at Fontley. He had

A striking portrait of Henry Cort. The unknown artist has captured the visionary genius of this essentially simple man whose 'one brilliant idea was exploited by others more cynical and worldly wise than himself'.

found a backer — Samuel Jellicoe, a friend from Cort's youthful days as a navy agent in London, had interested his father Adam Jellicoe in the Fontley forge. Adam Jellicoe gave every outward indication of being a man of some substance. He held the high position of Deputy Paymaster of Seamen's Wages and readily agreed to support the Fontley experiment. By 1781 he had invested the huge sum — for those times — of £27,000 and the business was known as Cort and Jellicoe.

In 1783 as a result of his work at Fontley, Cort took out the first of his patents for his new iron-manufacturing process. It was for a "peculiar method of preparing, welding and working various sorts of iron and reducing the same into uses by machinery, a furnace and other apparatus adapted and applied to the same purposes". One year later a second patent protected "a new mode of shingling, welding and manufacturing iron and steel into bars, plates, rods, etc., and otherwise of purer quality in large quantities by a more effective application of fires and machinery with a greater yield than any method before attained or put into practice". The new methods these patents protected were to have a great impact upon the centuries-old English iron industry. The Navy Board was especially interested in these patents. Cort sent it a sample bar of the high-quality iron produced by the new methods in July 1784 and the Board responded favourably:

> *Mr. Cort,*
>
> *We have received yr Lr of yesterday with a bar*
> *of Iron made of Ballast Iron wh you inform us can also be*
> *made from Shot, Shells, etc., and desire you will make*
> *your proposal for working up ye difft sorts of old iron in ye*
> *King's Yards for difft uses. We approve much of*
> *the bar and shall treat with you if your terms are*
> *reasonable.*
>
> *Charles Middleton, J. Williams, George Marsh.*

In 1787, the Board decided to use Cort's iron in the

Cort's forge at Fontley where he conducted his five-year-long experiment into the iron puddling process. The river Meon running alongside the forge provided the motive power for a huge tilt hammer.

navy and the naval dockyards. Up until then almost all the iron for naval use had been supplied by one major contractor, Anders Lindgren, who imported quantities of the iron known colloquially as Orground, from its source at Ôregrund in the province of Uppsala, Sweden. Now the Cort and Jellicoe enterprise was acknowledged as the pioneer in what may be termed the New Iron Industry. Cort could take credit for the rapidly diminishing imports of both Russian and Swedish iron as his methods became widely adopted by ironmasters around the country.

A few figures will put Cort's achievement in perspective. In 1740, the year of his birth, the English iron industry produced little more than 17,000 tons of iron a year. In 1789, five years after his patents, it reached 68,000 tons and in 1806 the total figure surpassed 250,000 tons. Cort's methods for the production of this superior-quality iron involved the system known as "puddling". Two furnaces, both heated by ordinary coal, were used. Pig iron from a blast furnace was transferred to a second furnace. Through doors in this second furnace, workmen puddled the metal by stirring it until it was in huge, malleable lumps called "loops". These were reheated and passed through huge rollers that removed impurities and left a high-quality, easily workable product.

All then seemed well. Cort's forge at Gosport provided the iron goods and equipment for Portsmouth dockyard and his time and energies were taken up with advising and giving particular assistance to other ironmasters and their workers. It appears from contemporary writings that these were in general a breed of men as hard as their product. They were slow to appreciate Cort's considerable expertise and the revolutionary effect his scientific and enquiring mind was to have both on their industry and their profits. A letter written in 1784 by James Watt of steam-engine fame was to prove prophetic: "Mr Cort has as you observe, been most illiberally treated by the trade; they are ignorant brutes yet they will contrive by some dirty evasion to use his process or such parts as they like, without acknowledging him in it." The "ignorant brutes", however, were not slow to pocket the profits — which

Many of the scenes depicted by the artist Joseph Wright date from the
early years of the industrial revolution. This rather romantic picture of an
iron-founder and his family shows a good rendering of a tilt-hammer at
work. It was painted in 1772. the year in which Henry Cort took over
Thomas Morgan's contract to supply the Dockyard with their iron
mooring chain.

were enhanced when the royalty they paid of ten shillings per ton was halved.

In 1789 the bottom dropped out of Cort's business world. Adam Jellicoe died suddenly and investigations into his financial position revealed that he owed his employers, the Navy Board, nearly £40,000. Cort had given his patents and half of his stock and profits to Adam Jellicoe as security and as partners in business they were responsible for each other's debts. The Navy Board seized all Cort's assets, his contracts were taken over, and all royalty payments ceased. Cort was declared bankrupt and his businesses at Fontley and Gosport were taken over by, of all people, Samuel Jellicoe, son of the disgraced Adam. There is evidence that the Gosport gentry were glad to see the back of Henry Cort. The by-products of his forge on The Green had caused environmental problems. Huge deposits of clinkers and ashes had had to be regularly cleared from the streets and on many occasions he had been threatened with prosecution by the local Watch Committee. At rural Fontley, the space problem was less acute. Here the forge and mill were operational as late as 1852, but on a drastically reduced scale, or, as one observer remarked in that year: "two old men, each probably over 80 years of age, were the solitary workmen...the following year the two ancient craftsmen either ceased their labours or went over to the majority and Fontley was now no longer known as a foundry".

Cort spent his last years in poverty and not until 1794 did he receive a state pension of £200 a year after an appeal to William Pitt. The petition accompanying the appeal refers proudly to him as "the father of the British iron trade". At this time, England had embarked on its long series of wars with France and Cort's innovations contributed towards the eventual outcome of the conflict between the two nations. Cort died in 1800, still in a state of genteel poverty, having struggled to support a wife and twelve children on his state pension. The desperate financial straits of Cort's widow and children were brought to the attention of the country's wealthy ironmasters, but a collection taken among them in

1811 realized only £871.

Realistically, of course, Cort's forges at Fontley and Gosport could not have developed further because the burgeoning iron industry needed to move to areas of Britain where coal and ironstone was in abundance. It was the ironmasters of the coal-rich Midlands who capitalized on Cort's inventions. Cort's processes were superseded in the mid-19th century by the Bessemer method of iron and steel production, named after Sir Henry Bessemer (1813-98).

Although Henry Cort played a key role — some would say the major role — in Britain's technological advances in both light and heavy industry, no fitting memorial exists to him in either Fareham or Gosport. He appears only in a corner of the frieze over the entrance to the Gosport Museum in Walpole Road and Fareham has the Henry Cort comprehensive school and a road — Cort Way — named after him. As memorials to a man who changed the whole direction of modern industry, these cannot be enough.

CHAPTER FIVE
Sea and Quay

The most eye-catching feature of Fareham's Borough shield is a sailing-ship — an appropriate reminder of Fareham's strong links with the sea. Today a large part of the waterfront maintains a low profile, almost unnoticed by the motorist caught up in a permanent traffic tangle at the approaches to the town centre. But in the more peaceful days of former centuries ships and boats of all types regularly negotiated a careful pathway from Portsmouth Harbour through Fareham Lake and Heavy Reach, past Cams Bay, and up to Lower Town, and Upper Quays to exchange merchandise such as coal, corn, salt, and hides for the local products of timber, bricks, pottery, leather, grain, and whiting for clay pipes. In those far-off times, when railways were unknown, and hazardous, unmade roads made heavy haulage well-nigh impossible, water communications were a tremendous advantage to Fareham's rise as a market town. Fareham's farmers and early industrialists thrived as cargo boats made their slow way to and from Dorset, the Isle of Wight, Devon, Kent, and London. That familiar, battered relic at the Quay today, the *Hexhamshire Lass*, reminds us that coal was once brought all the way from the Newcastle and Durham areas. Today, the ubiquitous lorry carries the goods that keep business brisk and consumers content — but at grim cost to the environment and public safety and well-being.

Water, — stream, river, or sea — always enhances a town. In Fareham, near the Quays, earlier residents of such houses as Belvoir, Elm Villa, and Southfield enjoyed a view of the water as yet unsullied by traffic. At elegant summer-afternoon garden parties at Cams Hall, ladies and gentlemen gazed at the tranquil seascape from the terrace.

A fine F.G.O. Stuart postcard view of a quiet and contemplative scene.
This was Fareham Creek in 1906.

Cams Hall once had its own private bathing-house at the northern end of a fine avenue of oaks and elms known as Bathing House Grove. In the early years of Victoria's reign bathing for pleasure and health was very much in vogue. Just across this part of the upper reach of Fareham Creek, an enterprising group of local businessmen came together in 1836 to build a sea-water bathing-house at a cost of £5,600. This exciting new establishment comprised separate large baths for men and women (mixed bathing was of course not considered respectable in those days) supplied at high water from the creek itself, together with hot and cold shower baths. The popularity of this new amenity led to a change of name for the tree-lined road upon which it was situated — originally known as Park Lane, it became known locally as Bathing House Lane and eventually Bath Lane. So popular was sea-bathing in this period that the author of the Fareham section of Mudie's guide-book to Hampshire of 1840 made special mention of it: "Portsdown shelters it [Fareham] from the east and north-east winds and the force of the south-west winds is also much broken. Hence the air has all the freshness of a sea one without any of its fury and consequently Fareham is a most advantageous place of resort for those who wish to enjoy the advantage of sea-bathing."

Today Fareham families tend to take their bathing pleasures in the comfort of the swimming pools in the Fareham Leisure Centre in a different Park Lane.

Sailing for pleasure is another popular activity in areas where water abounds. Fareham has had a thriving sailing club for many years. Regattas, once held in and around the creek at quite frequent intervals, were attractive and popular. These entertainments were not confined to sailing and rowing, but also included diving and swimming races and, on land, traditional old-English sports such as three-legged races, tilting the bucket, and climbing the greasy pole. Often the regatta evenings were enhanced by illuminated processions of boats and superb firework displays. In the early 19th century the annual St. Peter's and St. Paul's Fair, held on 29 and 30 June, also concluded with water sports. Tradi-

Local photographer Sidney Smith took this picture of the placid waters of Lower Quay in 1930. Among the buildings are Thomas' Grain Merchants, Fareham Flour Mills and Fred Dyke's Quayside Garage & Repair Shop.

tion has it that water sports of a less skilful kind were encouraged annually on the evening before the Fair, when the mill pond was completely drained to allow anyone who so desired to splash around in the muddy bed in the hope of collecting the struggling eels and fish.

Mention of the mill pond recalls the famous Cams Mill, which stood on the site of an earlier one mentioned in the Domesday Book. This old and picturesque building, which in its declining years saw the development of both a main road and a railway viaduct in its immediate vicinity, was photographed for picture postcards and sketched and painted by many, including that notable local water-colourist Martin Snape. It was demolished in 1920 and today the area is simply part of a vast traffic complex. It might, though, have been very different. Just after the First World War, Fareham councillor Charles Senior worked out a fine plan for a modern amenity at Bridgefoot, where the River Wallington joins Fareham Creek. His idea was that the water could be dammed at this point, thus turning the northern end of the creek into a lake. Boating facilities could be provided and the whole area would abound with beautiful pleasure gardens and walks. But, as F.C.E. Thurlow described in an article on Fareham in the *Hampshire* magazine, this enterprising local idea fell victim to the government's post-war spending cuts — the Geddes' Axe.

Proximity to the sea tends to encourage boat-building and its associated trades and crafts, and Fareham is no exception. In times of war, governments have always been mindful of the value of the nation's ports and places such as Fareham around the coasts have often been required to use their local talents in building and sailing boats as well as supplying men and equipment. Much of the timber for early wooden vessels came from Fareham Park and Titchfield Park, which supplied Chatham and other dockyards. In 1535 one James Hawkysworth wrote to John Dudley, Viscount Lisle, Sheriff of Hampshire: "Your ship sailed from Fareham on Sunday 26th September. Has sent in her 7000 of Tayl wood and a great ox from the prior of Christchurch; anchor stocks with a piece of

ash to make axles of; a hogshead of salt." Three years later
Lord Lisle received news from Sir Antony Windsor: "As to
your great wood you wrote for, there is a thousand readily
tallied in Farahame Park and a thousand more shall be ready
shortly, and then your warrant is expired. I would advise you
to make suit to my Lord of Winchester to have a quantity of
wood each year, for there is a new woddward, a servant of Sir
William Paulet...."

The earliest surviving record of shipbuilding at Fareham is dated 13 October 1403; from it we learn that a ship
named *Marie* was to be made ready by the end of the month
for Henry IV. Over two centuries later, in 1634, the ill-fated
Charles I, hard pressed for money as a result of wars with
Spain and France, introduced the tax known as "ship money".
Fareham had to pay £50 ship money in 1636 and in addition,
two years later, was required to provide a ship of 400 tons
and a company of 160 men to be ready within four months.

The beginning of the 19th century saw a large increase in naval activity and movements in the Fareham area,
largely on account of the Napoleonic Wars. Major naval
campaigns were an important feature of the struggle between
England and France. Many captured French ships were towed
into various parts of Portsmouth Harbour and unhappy enemy
survivors were imprisoned in dismal and insanitary hulks or, if
they were more fortunate, in Portchester Castle or Forton
Prison. As many as eighteen prison hulks were moored in
Fareham Lake, including *Suffolk*, *Crown*, and *Vigilant*, and the
inmates of these miserable institutions numbered over 9,000
by the end of the war. It is thought that a primitive hospital
was set up at Lower Quay for very ill prisoners from the hulks
and from Portchester Castle and those who died were buried
nearby in what became known as "Hospital Field". A skeleton
discovered four feet down in clay and gravel by workmen
digging at the Quay in 1943 is thought to be the remains of
one of these unfortunates. Fareham folk looked upon the
prisoners with a mixture of emotions. Many were fearful that
Fareham would be decimated through the spread of the various illnesses suffered by the prisoners but others were fasci-

nated to stare at these the only foreigners that they would ever see in their lives, and some were delighted to buy for a penny or two the combs which some of the prisoners made out of the bones left behind from their meals.

Fareham was responsible, largely through the Burrell and Fitchett families, for building some ships, including sloops, for the war, but the majority of the vessels produced locally at this time were trading ships of up to 200 tons. The increase in shipbuilding brought with it associated trades such as sail-making and rope-making.

One man who later became involved with boats as an amateur was the Rev. Edward Lyon Berthon who was vicar of Holy Trinity church from 1847 to 1855. Berthon was one of those energetic churchmen-visionaries of the mid-Victorian period who seemed able to cram a tremendous amount into one life. He studied medicine and theology, travelled far and wide, and worked on maritime experiments in his spare moments. He invented a folding or collapsible lifeboat, which was demonstrated before Queen Victoria at Netley. Berthon's boats were later carried in expeditions to the Arctic and were also supplied to General Gordon of Khartoum.

Fareham has maintained its close links with the Royal Navy during the 20th century. One of its most famous sons is Lt. Commander Leonard Fox. As captain of HMS *Mary Rose* during the First World War, he took part in the Battle of Jutland. But in 1917, as *Mary Rose* was leading a convoy of Norwegian merchant ships, she was attacked by enemy cruisers. After a fierce battle, *Mary Rose* was sunk. Only six of its crew survived. Fox was not among them. The Admiralty paid him this tribute: "He held on unflinchingly...he died leaving in the annals of his service an episode not less glorious than that in which Sir Richard Greville perished."

One result of the First World War was the appearance in 1923 of several German submarines, captured during hostilities, which had finally been brought up to Fareham to be broken up. To the great annoyance of local fishermen,

when the submarines were taken apart there was a good deal
of fuel spillage, which polluted the creek for several years.
After the Second World War, certain vessels of the reserve fleet
were laid up in Fareham Lake. Probably the last vessel specifi-
cally built for war to be seen in the Lake was the submarine
P556 which lay, a damaged and vandalized eyesore, exposed
at low tide for nearly twenty years until it was removed to
Tipnor.

In more recent years, Fareham's waterside has not
always been as tranquil as it looks. As the town's population
grew considerably during the 1960s and 1970s the problem of
sewage reared its ugly and odiferous head. The original
Salterns sewage works was found to be inadequate for the
growing demands of the town, and before rebuilding and
improvements were completed there were many complaints
about the smell and the condition of the waters in the creek.
When over a hundred residents embarked on a campaign to
clean up the creek in 1973, heaps of rubbish — including old
bicycles, exhaust pipes, car tyres, and large boulders — were
discovered and retrieved. A local doctor, despite wearing
protective gloves, received a cut on his thumb from a sharp
spike and suffered a serious infection. This incident focused
attention on the polluted waters, where, it was claimed, dan-
gerous organisms were growing apace in the mud from dis-
charged sewage. In the spring of 1974, a dredger engineer
who had been fishing in the creek reported that he had seen
eels dying and crabs climbing on top of one another to try to
escape from the water. Such revelations, together with the
regular horrible smell of acetone and ammonia and the discovery that the oxygen content of the water was too low to
support marine life, marked the nadir of the creek's fortunes.
But the sewage improvements at Salterns were soon in hand
and by early 1975 the creek was becoming cleaner, although
it was to be 1980 before the years of pouring treated effluent
into the water was ended as the sewage was finally diverted to
the Peel Common works, with the Salterns outflow now used
for storm water only.

New controversies arose during the 1970s. A fresh

proposal to dam the creek and provide a marina for 400 yachts was made in 1975. Objections were raised by the Fareham Sailing and Motor Boat Club who, having just cel-ebrated their 125th birthday with a week of racing and a carnival, claimed that this new marina would limit the pleas-ant sailing activities that had been the privilege of local people for so many years. Others feared that damming would result in the disappearance of water exchange and subsequent dam-age to the natural ecology of the waters. A consortium headed by round-the-world sailor Robin Knox-Johnson pressed hard for the marina idea and also considered building a wall across Cams Bay to provide a marina lake. In November 1975 the marina schemes were hotly debated by Fareham Council and scuttled by the narrowest of margins — one vote. So Fareham did not get its marina. Many were disappointed, but many others glad that, to quote from an excellent article by Lee Winnicott in *The Hampshire Telegraph*, "here the atmos-phere is more of a tiny village afloat than of the organised, streamlined and often competitive nature common to so many maritime and yacht centres."

In 1982, 1983, and 1984 the creek again enjoyed regattas organized by the Fareham Sailing and Motor Boat Club. The revival of this event in 1982, appropriately Mari-time England Year, attracted large crowds. The regattas of the next two years were just as enjoyable, but there was disap-pointment in 1985 when the club regretfully announced that there would be no more regattas — the event had become too much of a headache to organize.

way Station
Fareham

The railway station at Fareham in Edwardian days. A train has just
pulled in to the island platform, this was added to the station in 1889 to
handle traffic on the new line to Netley. There was once a separate
entrance-gate to the island platform reached by steps from the pavement
beneath the road bridge. Note the profusion of enamelled signs along the
bridge parapet and the elegant signalling system.

CHAPTER SIX
One Way or Another

One of the greatest difficulties facing the major areas of southeast Hampshire is that of too much traffic trying to use inadequate roads. The modern, socially conscious Fareham resident, gloomily contemplating the worsening problem of road travel in almost any direction, ponders the question, "Where did we go wrong?" Surely driving one's own car was once a positive pleasure?

There was once a time when the one advantage of owning a car — to be able to travel where and when you liked unhindered by other people — was not offset by the dangers and difficulties of today. But such a time was longer ago than we sometimes realize. Even in the 1930s letters to local news-papers complained about the difficulty of travelling from Gos-port to Portsmouth because of the delays in Fareham. Since the Second World War, Fareham has seen many road changes and schemes for improvement. But these roundabouts, fly-overs, road widenings, and one-way systems have brought only temporary respite before the traffic overwhelms them in its invincible advance. Meanwhile, the attempts to improve the traffic flow have altered Fareham's approaches beyond all recognition, always to their detriment, and in some areas, where houses are virtually surrounded by noisy, dirty roads, have created disruption and discomfort to the residents.

A profile survey of this area undertaken by Dr. Colin Mason and Dr. Steven Pinch of Southampton University in 1985 showed that 4,500 people commuted to Gosport from Fareham each day by car, with 3,500 doing the same from Gosport to Fareham. Such figures, added to the large amounts of shopping and lorry traffic, make it incredible that Fareham

This well-dressed assemblage of local people, including policemen, L.S.W.R.
staff and soldiers (with regimental mascot) are eagerly awaiting the
arrival at Fareham of Princess Henry of Battenburg (formerly Princess
Beatrice) who was paying an official visit to Fareham in October 1905.
Widowed for nine years, this popular princess, Victoria's youngest
daughter, had succeeded her husband Prince Henry as Governor of the Isle
of Wight.

has no rail passenger link with Gosport, and has not had one since as long ago as 1953. But things might have been even worse. If the 1983 Serpell Report on railways had been implemented, Fareham itself would have been without a station. Fortunately belated realization that public transport has a vital part to play in the communication links of today and tomorrow should ensure that Fareham will be able to maintain and improve its rail connections with the rest of the country.

Looking back at the history of transport and communication in Fareham may furnish us with some clues to the present difficulties. In the early 19th century Fareham was still a compact unit. Various turnpike trusts had already provided well-made toll roads, usually in good repair, into and out of the town. But the roads were not exactly teeming with traffic. Many people travelled no further than a few miles during their lifetimes. The typical citizen of, say, the 1830s lived, played, and worked almost exclusively within the Fareham community. Stagecoach services offered the chance of communication with the wider world, but few except the rich could afford them. Nor were stagecoach journeys pleasurable experiences. From Fareham to London, the journey could take anything up to eight hours and involve up to half-a-dozen changes of horses. Passengers paid a pound to be cramped together with others inside the stuffy coach, or approximately half-price if they dared brave the elements outside. The ride was unpredictable and the possibility of robberies ever-present. Accidents were not infrequent and could have unpleasant consequences — in 1810, for example, a passenger suffered a broken leg after a heavily overloaded coach overturned on the road between Gosport and Fareham.

The England of the early Victorians was about to be revolutionized by the appearance of a new transport system. First devised as a much more speedy alternative to canals and roads for the transport of goods and produce, the new network of steam railways which snaked across the country with amazing rapidity during the 1840s soon developed into a vast system for carrying passengers. The railways reached Fare-

An early twentieth-century view of the Red Lion Hotel's own 'courtesy coach' about to despatch a customer back to the railway station at the opposite end of West Street. On the other side of West Street can be seen the chemist's shop of Batchelor & Son, established since the middle part of the previous century.

ham in 1841 when the London and South-Western Railway
Company, having completed the line from London to
Southampton, extended a branch from Bishopstoke (now
Eastleigh) via Botley to Fareham and Gosport. The chief
engineer of the L.S.W.R., Joseph Locke, appointed Thomas
Brassey as contractor for the fifteen-mile stretch. Soon sleepy
Fareham awoke to the sound and sight of the "navvies" cutting and tunnelling a straight course through the countryside.
Fareham station was built unobtrusively at the end of West
Street — not as grand as the terminal station at Gosport, but
elegant enough — complete with a neat bridge leading the
line over the Southampton Road. Soon the inevitable railway
hotel was constructed near the station and by November 1841
everything was ready. The first trains rattled along the lines,
causing exhilaration to some and apprehension to others.

But before the novelty had time to wear off, a serious
problem arose. Fareham tunnel was unstable. While it was
under construction the engineers had discovered what railway
historian O.S. Nock has called "a soil that defied all theory...in
dry weather it was hard enough to need blasting, yet after
rain it became little better than very fluid mud." Various
methods had been employed to try to make the tunnel stable,
but the chief inspecting officer of the Board Of Trade, who had,
as required by law, inspected the whole line before its opening,
in his report laid the responsibility for the tunnel's safety on
the railway's chief engineer. As a result of this lack of confidence the Fareham line was closed only four days after it
opened. After many tests and experiments, it was decided that
the tunnel was safe and the line was re-opened on 7 February
1842. Anxiety about the safety of the tunnel must have
persisted, however, because eventually in 1904 a diversion
was constructed.

In the 1840s some Fareham residents saw the coming of the railway as an unwelcome intrusion, bringing with it
a sense of the unknown into their hitherto predictable lives.
But those with a wider imagination soon realized that besides
providing the opportunity to travel more quickly to distant
places, the railway would also facilitate the speedy dispatch of

31. RED LION HOTEL. FAREHAM. SIDNEY SMITH Photographer.

A fine 1930s photograph, again of the Red Lion, complete with its mock-Tudor frontage. The large circular disc on the far right-hand side of the building is an early AA road sign giving the distances to Southampton, Portsmouth and London.

farm and manufacturing produce from Fareham to more
numerous and more varied markets. It was not long before
Fareham became a junction station. The L.S.W.R. decided to
extend a line from the town eastwards to Portchester and
Cosham, there to connect with an extension into Portsmouth
from London via Worthing and Chichester (the direct line from
Portsmouth to London was still some years in the future). The
new scheme altered Fareham's landscape irrevocably, for it
involved carrying the railway out of the station on a high
embankment and then across the upper reaches of the creek
over a fine series of many-arched viaducts. The new line ran
parallel to West Street before bridging the water and then
passed Downend Farm and went under Downend Lane on its
way to Portchester. There, a spectacular brick and flint station was built in the style of a castle to reflect the village's
connection with its Roman fortress.

The new lines at Fareham proved to be both successful and profitable. Soon there were plans for further lines in
the area. In 1863 a branch was built from Gosport to Stokes
Bay and a triangular junction was provided so that trains from
Fareham could travel directly to Stokes Bay (the line was
closed in 1915). From the rail terminus on Stokes Bay pier a
new steamship service for Ryde on the Isle of Wight was
inaugurated, giving Fareham residents a quick holiday route to
the island.

During the first quarter century of Victoria's reign,
rail travel for leisure and pleasure was increasing. Fears
initially expressed by Jeremiahs — such as the doctor who
claimed that the body would disintegrate if exposed to speeds
of over 30 miles per hour — were soon discredited. The fact
that the queen was known to enjoy rail travel, and indeed had
often passed through Fareham station on her way to Gosport
for embarkation to her favourite home on the Isle of Wight,
added to the railway's popularity. Excursions were organized,
notably to the Great Exhibition of 1851, when many Fareham
people took the train to the capital to gaze in wonder for the
first time at the sights and sounds of a great city. Fares were
reasonably cheap — the Railways Act of 1844 compelled the

The eastern part of West Street photographed by F.G.O. Stuart before the First World War. The generous thoroughfare is as yet unsullied by motor traffic but there is a good selection of horse-drawn vehicles, from the grand and well-groomed to the small and humble. The building on the left is the Market (later Parish) Hall built in 1846 by a local subscription of £5 shares. Beyond that is the old fire station built on the site of Price's School.

railway companies to run at least one train every weekday (the "parliamentary trains") at fares not exceeding a penny a mile for adults and a halfpenny for children. Moreover, the L.S.W.R. had improved its carriage stock so much that even third-class travel along local lines was described as "the finest in England".

Further railway development in the area ensured that Fareham station was a busy, bustling place by the first decade of the 20th century. After many delays, Fareham had been provided with a direct link to Southampton when a line was established to Netley via Swanwick and Bursledon in 1889. In 1903 the final important connection into Fareham was completed with the Meon Valley line, which ran through Knowle, Wickham, Droxford, West Meon, Privett, and other stations to Alton, and thence direct to London. The Meon Valley line proved very important to Fareham — it brought easier communication with the outlying villages both for passengers and farming produce.

Thus by 1905 Fareham was an important traffic centre, with an extended station providing trains along five major routes — to Southampton, Eastleigh, the Meon Valley, Gosport, and Portsmouth. But the next new lines to be laid were along the roads. These were the rails for the exciting new tramway system, powered by electricity conducted through overhead wires. Gosport had had a horse-drawn tram system for several years, but the tram company, Provincial, now decided to electrify and to extend their network to Fareham. A power station, with a 160-foot chimney, as built at Hoeford. Soon the lines were being laid and the wires strung from the hard at Gosport, through Brockhurst, skirting Fareham Creek, passing under the railway viaduct, up Portland Street into West Street, and on to the terminus at the railway station. The first tram was driven on a trial run from Fareham to Gosport in December 1905 by John Fereday-Glenn. The regular service between the two towns opened on 24 January 1906, with driver Bob Heath and his conductor Jim May making the first of many thousands of journeys.

Tram no.16 approaches the corner into Portland Street on its journey to Gosport Hard in a post-First World War view of West Street. Thackeray's grandmother lived in the cottage on the right next to the Wesleyan Methodist church, both buildings now demolished to make way for the bus station.

Travel on one of the fleet of twenty-two trams may not have been the last word in comfort, but the painting and lettering upon the trams were works of art, so typical of the pride in public transport shown by both owners and the general public in those days. The trams were emerald green and cream, with the legend "Gosport and Fareham Tramways" painted on the rocker-boxes in black lettering with red shading. At both front and rear each tram carried a central light, a neat destination-board box, and its fleet number, stylishly displayed. We can see, too, from several surviving postcards and photographs showing Fareham and Gosport street scenes that the trams were maintained in excellent condition. Although passengers forced to go up the winding stairs to sit on the top deck in the winter must have cursed their luck, in the summer they must have enjoyed an exhilarating ride and a grand view, as do their modern counterparts on Provincial's summertime open-top bus services. But the drivers, like their predecessors on the stagecoaches and the early locomotives, were hardy souls who had to brave the elements with little protection. The trams ran every fifteen minutes and the early fares were fourpence single and sixpence return from Fareham to Gosport Hard. Soon the frequency of the service and the advantage that the trams went right into Gosport — unlike the trains, which put you down at the terminus with still a considerable amount of walking to do to get into the town — began to attract passengers away from railway between the two towns.

Gosport railway station, at Garden Lane, was though, reasonably convenient for the schoolchildren of the new grammar school in Clarence Road. Many pupils travelled in by train from Fareham, Botley, Funtley, and even Havant. One girl, writing an account of "The Joys of Being a Train-girl" in the school magazine in 1916, has left an amusing picture of Fareham station: "It is quite a usual thing in the morning to find six green-capped girls in a group beyond the bookstall, their satchels piled on the seat behind them. If it is cold a move is made to the other end of the platform, where three or four pillars and a long seat serve admirably for a game of tag (the waiting rooms are being swept out and we are not al-

Fareham bus station as it appeared in the 30s and 40s. The Wesleyan chapel still managing to cling on to its prime position at the heart of the busy commercial centre.

lowed inside). By the time the down train runs in we are quite warm and ready to "do our bit". This "bit" is looked upon in various degrees of gratitude by the railway officials. Porters are so few in number that it takes quite a long time to move the luggage. We have never been told we are in the way, but much depends on the nature of the guard or whether the porters are hurried. Milk churns we are naturally not allowed to touch. Only once did we attempt to move a barrel, the contents of which were at first a mystery. Curiosity overcame us, so we made a tiny hole in the wet cloth cover, thus disclosing some small mackerel. It was with abated zeal we rolled that tub, and, alas, the hole got larger and at each twist a slippery fish slid to the platform...."

As yet of course it was only public transport that had any great effect on Fareham's traffic. Perhaps Monday market day was an exception, when various horse and pony-drawn conveyances, together with the herds of animals on their way to be bought or sold, made local people glad that West Street was a wide thoroughfare. Many Edwardian picture-postcard views of West Street show people of all ages happily ambling along in the middle of the road, with the odd tram or horse and cart for company, the whole scene framed by the tall question-mark lamp standards and the elegant supporting-frames of the overhead wires among the well-kept trees. The scenes often have the appearance of waiting for road transport to begin in earnest — a stage set without the actors. But Fareham's trim roads did not have to wait long for the internal-combustion engine to shatter their peace forever. As early as 1895, local people witnessed with much excitement the brief but eventful appearance of one of the very earliest petrol-engined horseless carriages. A Mr. J. Kooson of Southsea imported a Lutzmann car from Germany and his wife wrote about their adventures in her diary. Here are some extracts:

Dec. 9, 1895. Drove to Lee at 10. Motor sparked at once and went well. After lunch, started for home, came round by Fareham, had lovely drive; police spotted us; awful crowd followed us at Cosham; had to beat them off with umbrella.

A close-up view of tram no.16 (as seen on page 94) when new in 1906.
It was captured at the Hoeford depot just before commencing duty on the
newly electrified route between Gosport and Bury Cross. The tram could
seat 55 people, most of whom would presumably want to be downstairs in
the winter and on the top deck on fine summer days.

> *Dec. 10. Policeman called at 1.30, took our names*
> *re. driving through Fareham without red flag ahead.*
>
> *Dec. 16. Took train to Fareham, met Hobbs [solicitor]*
> *and proceeded to Court House. Filthy place. Hobbs*
> *spoke up well for motors. Silly old magistrate fined us*
> *one shilling and costs, 15s-7d.*

Despite this inauspicious debut, the motor car was soon here to stay. E. and C. Hunt's large cycle shop in High Street was selling Pratt's motor spirit by 1905 and the Red Lion Hotel provided petrol soon afterwards. As yet, however, motor cars were not within the range of the average person's purchasing power. The first major intrusion into the scene from the internal-combustion engine was the rapid development of bus services after the First World War. The volume of exhaust fumes rose further after Provincial ran its last electric tram on 31 December 1929, dug up the tracks, and went over to buses. The motor bus had an obvious advantage over the tram in that, being unrestricted by tracks, it was able to take on many more different routes. Buses reached a wider range of villages and people. During the 1920s many bus companies sprang up in the area — Enterprise, Smith Brothers, Mallard's and Moore's among others — all vying for custom and sometimes racing for customers against each other in and among the Provincial trams. Inevitably over the years the larger companies — Hants & Dorset, Southdown, and Provincial — swallowed up the enterprising smaller local firms but not before each had contributed some folklore to local history.

As the roads began to fill with buses and private cars, the railways, once the only way to travel, began to decline, at first imperceptibly but then steeply. The Second World War saw renewed activity at local stations, as a result mainly of evacuation. But peace brought in its wake a period of shortage and rationalization. Economies were enforced, and the railways began to decline. Soon Fareham's routes, so long taken for granted, began to appear luxuries. With very little protest from local people, British Railways closed down the

West Street in the 1930s. On the left is the old-established business of Herbert Pyle the baker, who arrived in Fareham in 1883 to join his uncle and later branched out on his own at these premises. Prior to this it had been the Paragon Hotel and originally the site of one of Fareham's oldest inns, the White Hart.

passenger service between Fareham and Gosport in 1953, leaving the fine terminus to the mercies of rot, decay and vandalism. Just at a time when massive housing development was taking place between the two towns, no-one had the foresight to see what a burden this closure would place upon the roads within a very few years. Next line to go was the route through the Meon Valley, closed to passenger traffic on 5 February 1955, thus depriving Fareham of one of its most picturesque and useful routes. Ironically, one of the connecting routes to this line, the Alton to Alresford section, now enjoys thousands of visitors a year as the Watercress Line, one of the best preserved steam railways in the country. Few cared enough for such routes in the 1950s however. As *The Hampshire Chronicle* reported on 1 February 1955, "the Meon Valley railway, within a few days of its closure, is probably being visited by more people interested in railways than ever before in its history." During the final days there were two packed excursion trains from London to the Meon Valley Line for both rail enthusiasts and ramblers. In the 1980s the railways were not treated well either by the general public or by government, which provided little enough money for the railways while always bowing to every demand of the road lobby. Fareham station staff worked hard during the early 1980s to maintain a decent service. An arson attack on the station in March 1983 destroyed the ticket office and part of the platform roof. Hopefully, though, this was the nadir of local railway fortunes — afterwards there was a slow realization that the roads in the area had reached saturation point and that the railways had a large part to play in any transport scheme.

More money was eventually made available. After many years of discussion, British Rail at last decided to electrify the lines from Portsmouth to Southampton and Eastleigh, with the result that in the early 1990s the new Solent Link service provided, for the first time in half-a-century, a direct service to London. It was hoped by many that the Gala Day with which the new service was inaugurated would mark a rebirth of the age of the train at Fareham.

Some of the girls of Western House School in West Street take a break from instruction for this photograph taken in the early 1920s. The school changed both its site and its name — an earlier establishment in West Street was known as Orme Lodge School. Later still, in 1928, it found a new home in the High Street and became known as Wykeham House School under the headship of Miss Alsop.

CHAPTER SEVEN
Schools and Children

Fareham shares its educational history with that of the rest of the country. In England very little provision was made for teaching the children of those who could not afford to pay for education until the early years of the 19th century, when two voluntary societies, the National Society (sponsored by the Church of England) and the British and Foreign School Society (sponsored by the nonconformists) provided schools. In 1833 public money was granted for the first time to aid the societies in their work — the beginning of the state's involvement in education. In 1870 an Elementary Education Act put education more securely among the public services and instituted elected School Boards to provide new schools, or help existing ones, from the rates. The aim of these 19th-century schools was to produce basically literate and numerate working-class children with, of course, a knowledge of the Scriptures.

In Fareham, National and, later, Board schools were built in Wickham Road, Osborn Road, Gordon Road, and Harrison Road between the years 1850 and 1900. The little rural community at Funtley also had its school. Most of the children at these schools left at the age of eleven or twelve to work, like their fathers and mothers before them, in the brick-yards, the breweries, the tannery, the potteries, or the fields and farms of neighbouring villages. Many of the girls found jobs as servants in the well-to-do houses of Victorian Fareham.

Typical of Fareham's local-authority schools in the late-Victorian period was the Fareham Board School for Girls and Infants (later Fareham Country Primary School) in Wickham Road. The school opened its doors on 2 July 1877 to receive its first intake of thirteen infants, to be watched over

Fun and games for the privileged young men of Stubbington House School on a school sports day in the 1920s. It is interesting to note that not one of these boys has his 'stockings' around his ankles.

by headmistress Miss Mary Rich, and sixteen girls, welcomed by her opposite number in the girls' school, Miss Jane Bailey. The number of pupils grew steadily and dramatically, until in 1890 it had reached a total of 347 infants and girls. By this time the two headmistresses had been joined by monitresses, usually teenage girls hoping to become teachers themselves. When Fanny Bishop was appointed monitress in 1881 she was fourteen years old and was paid three shillings a week.

The school's early registers are of particular interest because they show the occupations of the children's parents, who, in 1877, included bricklayers, tanners, corn factors, and potters. There was also a sea captain, a tinman, and an asylum attendant — presumably from Knowle Hospital, which had opened in 1852. These parents paid twopence a week for each child, but poor families sometimes had great difficulty in raising this apparently modest sum from their weekly budgets. Fareham was no different from other small towns in the mid-Victorian period — although employment was widely available in the traditional trades, it was not well paid and many of the jobs were seasonal. The main source of finance for the schools was, however, not the parents payments but government capitation grants paid to the head teachers on the results of testing the children in the three Rs. Small wonder then that after education was made compulsory in 1880 the school registers reflect the teacher's concern when attendance figures dropped as they frequently did, through bad weather, sickness, or lack of adequate footwear.

However, all was not gloom and despondency. The daily life of the Board-school pupil had its lighter moments. Occasional treats and holidays punctuated the school year. Children put down their Marshall's Universal Readers and abandoned their slates and pencils for special treats, among them half-holidays for the numerous royal births, marriages, and deaths. Sports and country dancing around the maypole in Bath Lane recreation ground were much enjoyed, while the Fareham Regatta was an annual delight.

There were many other types of educational estab-

As the clouds of war gather once again over Europe, class VIII of Redlands
Lane Junior School assemble for their 1939 class photograph. The gas
masks are evidence of the horrors ahead and evacuation was a distinct
possibility, but these bright young faces seem fairly optimistic about the
whole thing. In the end the gas masks were not needed and thankfully
they did not have to suffer the upset of evacuation.

lishments in the town. Some of these were described as "private adventure schools". We read of a Miss Alston who, in a room measuring 12 ft. by 15 ft. furnished with two desks and forms, taught eleven children whose ages ranged between five and twelve. Mrs. Kempster in her one room, taught twenty-two children, the youngest of whom was one year old. Mrs. Ridlett squeezed thirty children into a room 12 ft. by 12 ft. These sound like Dickensian horrors to us today, but clearly there was a market for them as witness the numbers in attendance.

Other private schools — at what might be called the more genteel end of the market — were Miss Treadwell's school for girls in West Street, the Misses Turners' establishment in Hartlands Road, Miss Kiln's in Portland Street, and Miss Blake's in Gosport Road. Miss Treadwell's 1901 prospectus for her Milston High School makes interesting reading. It informs parents that girls are received from five years of age. Her "moderate terms" encompassed exercises and Swedish drill by Sergeant Sampson, while Madame Dunn came over from Southsea to instil into the older girls the arts of dressmaking, needlework, and cutting out. Miss Treadwell clearly had an eye to the new century and the Modern Woman — shorthand and typewriting were also in the curriculum, which prepared the older girls for the Oxford and Cambridge local examinations.

A well-regarded school for boys was Blenheim Lodge, known to have been flourishing well before 1867. By 1901 it had become the Blenheim House School and under its principal, Mr. R. Arnold, was a coeducational establishment operating in two semi-detached houses off West Street. Its large, airy dormitories were fitted throughout with electric light and Mr. Arnold promised "all home comforts" at an all-in rate of 10 guineas a term.

The Misses Porter for many years ran a coeducational school, St. Fillans, in Southampton Road. At Wallington, orphan children were cared for at St. Edith's Home for Waifs and Strays, where, in addition to spiritual and moral guidance,

A section of the pupils and staff at Wykeham House School in 1949. A contemporary girl pupil recalls that children were often in trouble for attempting to pick fruit from the bountiful harvest of the Kintyre House apple trees next door. Staff in this photograph include the Headmistress Miss G.A. Beer and Miss V. Jewell, Miss M. Cork, Miss E. Morris, Mrs. M. Burman, Miss K. Pond, Miss Cocks and Miss M. Buckler.

they were given basic instruction in the three Rs. In modern guise, St. Edith's is now the Roundabout Hotel, easily visible from the motorway.

Much the most prestigious school in Fareham, and the one that is forever associated with the town, is Price's or, to give it its full title, Price's Charity School. This was the gift to the town of William Price, a wealthy and philanthropic Fareham timber merchant. In his will, dated 1721, Price bequeathed his house in West Street, his estate at Crocker's Hill, and his farm lands at Elson, Gosport, to the minister and churchwardens of the parish of Fareham who, as trustees, were charged with establishing a charity school for thirty poor children of the parish in Price's old family home in West Street. The trustees promptly executed the charge laid upon them and the school flourished, supported by an annual allowance of 40 shillings per pupil "for the purchase of books and sea coals for firing". Price was a man of some substance and his will also decreed that any surplus from the rents on his properties should be distributed among deserving poor widows of the parish of Fareham.

Presumably the school was financed by the rents from Price's Fareham and Gosport properties. The master's salary in 1721 was fixed at £35 per annum with rent-free accommodation in the schoolhouse. One hundred years later it was raised to £52. It is interesting to compare this with Jane Bailey's remuneration as head of the Fareham Board School for Girls in Wickham Road, who had responsibility for 200 pupils. In 1877 she received £100 per annum, with no rent allowance.

Price's charity schoolchildren would have been easily distinguishable in their smart blue cloaks over uniforms of matching blue, their hats and shoes adorned with silver buttons and buckles. An annual entrance examination for the school was held on Ash Wednesday and success consisted simply of reading a passage from the Bible or prayer book to the satisfaction of the vicar or churchwardens.

Some charming competitors in fancy dress at Fontley fête, probably 1953.
The date can be guessed from the little Smith's crisps girl on the front row
with a Smith's logo on her skirt which seems to represent E II R. The
girl on the left has a necklace of liquorice sweets and a sign celebrating
their removal from the post-war ration list.

In 1846 William Price's now dilapidated house was dismantled and a new schoolhouse built in its stead. The school, which from this time on taught only boys, remained in this building until 1907, when the premises in Park Lane were opened.

Secondary education for girls in Fareham until the state grammar school opened in the 1950s was provided by Wykeham House School. The school first saw the light of day as Orme Lodge before the First World War, later emerged as Western House, and finally became Wykeham House, taking its name from the 14th-century Bishop of Winchester, William Wykeham, who was born in the nearby village of Wickham. "W.H.", as it was affectionately known, suffered mixed fortunes in its twenty years of existence but just before the Second World War it had over 200 pupils on its registers. The pupils' family backgrounds reflected the then largely rural nature of Fareham society. Farmers' daughters mingled with those of prominent tradesmen and business and professional men, many of whom were also engaged in agricultural concerns.

The 18th-century elegance of the handsome premises at 69 High Street reflected the tone of the education at this school, where good manners (inspired by Bishop William's motto Manners Makyth Man) consideration for others, and a sound grammar-school curriculum assured its success. Wykeham House must be one of only very few schools were on Monday mornings pupils often wended their way along the wide open spaces of West Street dodging animals en route to the market! Morning assembly was held in the beautiful conservatory-cum-garden room. The garden itself was an especial delight, high-walled and rich in fruit and flowers in the summer season. Elinor Brent-Dyer, author of the *Chalet School* books for girls, was a teacher at the school during its Western House phase; it would be pleasant to think that something of the Wykeham House ambience found its way into her stories.

Stubbington House School was in its heyday probably

The staff of Price's School gather to honour the retirement in 1959 of a popular headmaster — George Dalton, third from the right in the first standing row.

the most famous naval preparatory school in Britain. The school was founded in 1841 by the Reverend William Foster, vicar of Crofton, in the 18th-century Manor House of Stubbington. From an initial intake of ten boys the school progressed to over one hundred and fifty pupils in the late-Victorian period. The naval connection appears to have stemmed from the Reverend Foster's wife, who was a daughter of Admiral John Hayes. To read the early prospectuses of Stubbington House is to be transported to another world. The staff were prepared to receive the sons of noblemen and gentle-men and to equip them for careers in the navy and the professions. Senior pupils were supplied with wine and ale as extras. Optional subjects as diverse as chemistry, music, fencing, gymnastics, and rifle shooting were offered, a far cry indeed from the three Rs of the National and Board schools!

The school's list of Old Boys is like a roll-call of England's history. There are, of course, the seamen who are the school's principal claim to fame, the first of whom was Admiral "Lord Charles" Beresford, a Lord of the Admiralty and in 1902-03 and 1910-16 MP for Portsmouth. But there are also a fistful of other MPs, columns of soldiers, flights of air-men, a royal prince (Alexander Albert of Battenberg, Queen Victoria's grandson, later Marquess of Carisbrooke), and a much-loved Bishop of Portsmouth, the Right Reverend W.L.S. Fleming. Of all these figures, two stand out above the rest because their careers in very different ways reflect something of the particular ethos of this part of south Hampshire with its long tradition of seafaring. Robert Falcon Scott, who achieved posthumous world fame as Captain Scott of the Antarctic, was an Old Boy as was T.O.M. Sopwith, the aircraft designer and international yachtsman.

After the Second World War the school returned to Stubbington House from its evacuation to Cornwall, but finan-cial considerations dictated the school's 1960s move to Earleywood in Berkshire, where it flourishes today. All that remains of the original building in the village of Stubbington is the Assembly Hall, now used as a community centre.

A near neighbour to Stubbington House was the Seafield Park House School, established in 1890 by the Reverend Rupert William Pain, a close associate of the Foster family. The school was advertised as a college for the education of the sons of gentlemen, with the emphasis on a career in engineering. It seems to have run in tandem with Stubbington House and in its later years it had close associations with the Royal Navy, becoming the Admiralty's School for Artificer Apprentices in 1947.

CHAPTER EIGHT
Fareham at War 1939-45

The outbreak of the Second World War plunged rural Fareham and its villages into the thick of the war effort. Because of its geographical position at the head of Portsmouth Harbour Fareham was considered to be vulnerable to any invasion attempt by the German forces. Although, at the fall of France in July 1940, the service authorities went on the alert, these fears were fortunately unfounded. Another fear was that Luftwaffe pilots might jettison their bombs over Fareham between missions to strike at both Portsmouth and Southampton and in the event Fareham suffered its fair share of bombing.

In 1938, Fareham Urban District Council responded to the government's Air Raid Precautions Act by preparing its citizens for the mayhem to come. The delivery of Anderson shelters to every household took place in the spring of 1939, while public shelters of reinforced brick and concrete sprang up at strategic points. Ten of these were built in Fareham, nine in the immediate vicinity of West Street and one in High Street near the Golden Lion. The surrounding villages were thought to be equally liable to aerial attack. At Portchester a shelter with capacity for 500 people was built at Newtown, while Sarisbury and Titchfield had two each.

The responsibility for the running of these shelters was vested in the ARP, whose centre was established in 1939 in offices in Portland Chambers, close to the bus station. Rules for correct shelter behaviour today make amusing reading. It was an offence for a person to "enter or remain in a shelter if he is drunk or if his person or clothing is offensively unclean or verminous" or "by forcible or improper means to enter or seek to enter any sanitary convenience in or appurtenant to the

*During the Second World War, Fareham, as a potential enemy target, had
to play a major role in the organisation of local civil defence services and
at the same time try to free men for front line duty. Here a score of
smart policemen lead a parade of local firemen and other services along
West Street.*

shelter or knowingly intrude upon the privacy of a person using such a convenience". Firearms were not allowed in the shelters and smoking, singing, or playing a musical instrument were all offences. One group of shelter users, the schoolchildren, regularly disobeyed the injunction against singing.

Perhaps surprisingly, Fareham schoolchildren were not evacuated as were their counterparts in Portsmouth and Gosport. Both these towns were judged, rightly, to be extremely vulnerable to attack from the air because of the Royal Naval Dockyard and the many military and naval establishments around the harbour. It was one of the ironies of evacuation that Portsmouth and Gosport schoolchildren were found billets little more than a stone's throw from Fareham in the Meon Valley villages. So, when the sirens wailed during school hours Fareham's teachers led their charges into the candle-lit playground shelters. To keep them occupied and to take their minds off the aerial bombardment outside, the children were encouraged to sing and to recite poems as they sat on wooden benches ranged down each side of the shelter. Favourite shelter ditties were "Ten Green Bottles", "Run Rabbit Run", and "Roll Out the Barrel", all roared out fortissimo by the children in an effort to drown out the sound of the guns from nearby anti-aircraft batteries. All in all, teachers had tremendous responsibilities at this period, the chief of which was to keep up their own and the children's morale. Humour kept breaking through. Once a harassed young teacher from Redlands Lane Junior School was escorting her crocodile of juniors to the Tin Tabernacle in Mill Road — in use as an overspill classroom. An elderly passer-by enquired, "Are these children all yours?" and received the reply, "Yes, all mine, but all with different fathers".

The ARP wardens appeared everywhere and inspired confidence, but they did have their limitations. One 20 September 1940, this notice appeared on the noticeboard at the Portchester wardens' headquarters:

> *To All Group Wardens — Childbirth During Air Raids*
> *Should enquiries for assistance be made to wardens, it*

On a bright winter's morning early in the Second World War, local
defence volunteers put in some first-aid practice in readiness for possible
casualties. These back-up forces worked splendidly throughout the war to
help protect the civilian population.

is recommended that they get in touch with the nearest
midwife or doctor. Do not contact the first aid post
unless no other assistance is possible.
Resident midwives:
Nurse Dicker, 5, Mount View Avenue
Nurse Grundy, 10, Windsor Road
Mrs. Wallis, 152, White Hart Lane.

Although it suffered more lightly than either Portsmouth or Gosport, Fareham took its share of air raids. Between 7 June 1940 and 5 November 1944 the alert sounded 1,543 times. Twenty-two people were killed by enemy bombing, 59 were admitted to hospital: with moderate to serious injuries, and 119 sustained minor injuries. Seventy-nine houses were totally destroyed by bombing, 165 were badly damaged, and more than 4000 needed repair work, principally the replacement of windows and of tiles and chimney-pots. Townspeople unfortunate enough to be bombed out of their homes were given temporary refuge in rest centres. The largest of these was at Harrison Road Senior School. Others were set up at Portchester, in the Methodist Sunday School, the Senior School in White Hart Lane, and the Junior School in Castle Street. Similar provision was made for the people of the outlying villages. Warsash's Congregational Sunday School doubled as a rest centre while at Sarisbury the parish hall and the Senior School in Brook Lane were made available. Titchfield's Junior School provided temporary accommodation for one hundred people, who could take their meals at the Congregational Church Hall.

Fareham experienced its worst bombing on the night of 10/11 March 1941 when the Luftwaffe bombed Portsmouth and dropped hundreds of incendiaries on the neighbouring harbour towns. The bombing raids, terrifying though they were, provided one section of the population at least with an absorbing hobby. As the war progressed, Fareham schoolchildren, like many others up and down the country, vied with each other in adding to their shrapnel collections. One wartime Fareham schoolboy remembers that his own hoard included the tail fin of a German bomb complete with manufac-

During the war the 'Dig For Victory' campaign was supported by the joint efforts of many groups of local people and everyone was required to lend a hand. Here, an extended family group are lifting and bagging potatoes.

turer's markings.

Many of Fareham's larger houses were requisitioned
by the government for emergency war service. In 1940,
Fareham House in East Street was for six months the headquarters of the 35th Anti-Aircraft Brigade until it was transferred to Fort Fareham. The house was the operational centre
for the anti-aircraft defences for Portsmouth, Southampton,
and the Isle of Wight and its ground floor became the operations room in which enemy aircraft were plotted by a mixed
staff from all three services. The nearby Cedar tea rooms, on
the corner of Bath Lane, served as the unit's mess. This
attractive building in its setting of mature cedar trees later
became the shop and store of the Cedar Garage. The site is
now occupied by a block of flats.

In 1941 Cams Hall was requisitioned by the Admiralty to accommodate the manager of the engineering department's drawing-office staff, whose Dockyard premises had been
blitzed. The staff remained for the duration of the war in the
romantic surroundings of the Cams estate. Their work encompassed the maintenance, operation, and construction of naval
vessels in Portsmouth Dockyard, including battleships, cruisers,
destroyers, submarines, minesweepers, and fleet auxiliary
repair vessels, and related work for all establishments within
the Southern Command. Mindful that even Cams Hall might
not prove sacrosanct to German bombers, the Admiralty
ensured that the department was as self-sufficient as ingenuity
could make it. A generator was installed for emergency
lighting together with a fire-defence system and a separate
telephone switchboard. A car-ferry service maintained a
constant link between the drawing office and the Dockyard.
Most of the professional staff travelled in daily from Portsmouth by Southdown bus — season tickets supplied by the
Admiralty — but many of the cleaning and canteen staff were
from Fareham, as were the labourers who did a variety of
tasks in and around the building. A former tracer who
worked there during most of the war has the warmest memories of her time spent at Cams Hall. The grand surroundings
encouraged many amorous affairs amongst the youthful staff,

*In much the same way as the rest of the population was encouraged to
'Dig For Victory' farmers were encouraged to 'Plough For Victory'. With
many of the able-bodied men away on active service and with so much
extra land being taken into cultivation, the need for extra hands was dire.
Here, eight happy land-girls from a farm near Fareham, take a break from
their hard work to drum up some favourable publicity for their service.*

inflamed by the frequent opportunities to meet on the back stairs and the discreet cover provided by the woods for lunchtime dalliance. The extensive plantation of Cams also included a barrage-balloon site and — in the lead up to D-day — a large contingent of marine commandos.

In the autumn of 1943, the final build-up to the invasion of Europe began. The construction of the component parts of the Mulberry harbours took place along the coasts, principally at Stokes Bay, Browndown, and Hillhead. Vast numbers of workmen, many of them imported Irish labourers, were drafted into Fareham and Gosport for this purpose. In Fareham the Urban District Council staff were responsible for the provision of billets for these essential workers. Much of this billeting work and the feeding and clothing of the men was undertaken by the Women's Voluntary Service on behalf of the council, their operations directed from their headquarters at 86 West Street. Meals for all such essential workers were available at the British Restaurant, which had been established in 1940 at Westbury Road. These government-subsidized eating places came in for a good deal of bantering criticism, mainly on account of the basic nature of the meals served, but they were a godsend to service men and women and shift-workers who could get a hot meal for under a shilling and tea or coffee for twopence a cup.

Workers on the Mulberry harbours were carried to their workplace by courtesy of the Fareham and Gosport Omnibus Company for the construction period of about nine months to June 1944. In the last days of May, Fareham's highways and byways were crammed to bursting point with British and Commonwealth troops and their vehicles en route for the coasts and Southampton docks. Bath Lane recreation ground was the temporary camp for the men of the 1st Canadian Army, who were visited and wished Godspeed by King George VI. Many friendships were struck up during this period between the "invaders" and the "invaded". Local people, initially resentful of the vast military influx visited upon them, soon warmed to the cheerful young men on their doorsteps. Money, though, was a problem for the troops at this time.

Patriotic crowds line West Street to watch a morale boosting procession of local volunteer organisations. With their positive image and hard work, the land-girls clinging to this farmer's tractor could rightly share in the home front victory.

Their English currency had been exchanged for a special printing of French francs. Residents along the Wickham-Fareham road can remember soldiers offering to sell army blankets for the price of a round or two of drinks from the local pubs.

While the troops waited, their presence in the streets of Fareham was nightly obscured by noxious emission of thick, black oily smoke designed to render them invisible to German reconnaissance planes. The smoke was produced from special vehicles jocularly dubbed "fish-and-chip shops" by local school-children. It was harmless though evil smelling, but one nasty accident occurred when a Fareham schoolboy was run over and seriously injured by one of the smoke-producing vehicles.

Out at Warsash, things were on the move. HMS *Tormentor* was an important arm of the special Operations Executive. It shared its site at the mouth of the River Hamble with the Southampton University school of navigation. Here, men were trained to raid the French, Dutch, and Norwegian coasts and raiding parties left the Warsash shore nightly until June 1944. Warsash Sailing Club became the headquarters for the engineering officers and the local playing fields re-sounded to the exuberant shouts of multi-national rugby and football. The Rising Sun pub catered to the servicemens' thirsts while in the village hall the WVS were on hand to provide food and material comforts.

Fishing had always been a mainstay of the Warsash economy and the necessary security restrictions imposed upon access to the foreshore could have been damaging. The diffi-culty was partially resolved, and the fishermens' livelihoods to some extent protected, by issuing them with official passes. One totally unexpected bonus came the way of the villagers. Hundreds of American troops who were camped in the River Hamble area were consigning their superfluous food into the waters of the river. Soon, surprised and delighted locals were beachcombing for succulent hams and cheeses and other goodies brought in on the tide. Customs officials from Southampton turned a blind eye to this innocent if illegal

The girls of the Land Army came from many different backgrounds, few actually came from farming families. Three of the eight bicyclists captured earlier, help the war effort by picking tomatoes on a farm near Fareham.

pastime.

D-day did not put an end to the dangers facing the civilian population. The flying bomb or V1 burst upon the scene in the summer of 1944 just after the invasion forces left these shores. Many local people will recall the bomb which cut out over Stubbington village in June. One person was killed and the explosion put paid to the old blacksmith's forge, a shop, and the village post-office and the telephone exchange. Holy Roof Church was damaged and its east window — dedicated to the memory of Henry Peter Delmé of Cams Hall, High Sheriff of Hampshire in 1925 — was destroyed.

It was not only the men of Fareham who played their parts in the Second World War. Fareham women were employed making munitions at the Royal Naval Armament Depot at Priddy's Hard, Frater, and Bedenham. At the Clarence Yard victualling depot in Gosport and its outstation at Hoeford bus depot, women packed emergency rations and supplies for the armed forces. On the farms of Fareham and in the villages the workers of the Women's Land Army, in their jaunty hats, breeches, and thick stockings, were a familiar sight. They played a vital role in keeping the granaries full and producing fresh vegetables and fruit from the smallholdings. Fareham schoolchildren too were encouraged to cultivate vegetables and they also collected hundred of pounds of blackberries from the lanes and fields in the hot August days. This summer harvest was converted into jam and preserves to add variety and colour to the nutritious but boring wartime diet.

The war had its lighter moments. The government tried hard to keep up the spirits of the people. Its Holidays at Home appeal, inaugurated in 1942, discouraged people from travelling too far from their home patch at a time when fuel for public transport was desperately short. Fareham, in common with other towns up and down the country, cooperated by offering entertainment for stay-at-home townspeople. A Holidays at Home programme for 1943 survives to give us a flavour of the innocent pastimes devised for the people of Fareham during the month of August. For the sports enthusiast, a Grand Boxing Tournament at the Connaught Hall beckoned. At the Bath Lane recreation ground, the Hampshire Constabulary fielded a cricket team against the Portsmouth City Police and for a little later in the month, Jimmy Allen advertised his team of soccer professionals. Wallington was to have a Grand Fete with a Punch and Judy Show and no fewer than three Beauty Competitions — to find the bathing belle, the best coiffure, and the prettiest ankle — the 1940s were truly the vintage years of the Ankle Competition. A Bandaging Competition gave the voluntary organizations an opportunity to practise and demonstrate their skills and win a prize into the bargain for the best and fastest bit of bandaging. Elsewhere, music lovers were catered for with a Celebrity Concert at the Methodist Hall in King's Road. The opera singer Robert Easton was joined by "other artistes" for a musical evening, the proceeds of which went to local war charities. Grand Dances figured prominently in the Holidays at home programme. Throughout the period a cinema van was parked at the Bath Lane ground, showing morale-building films on the progress of the war.

Fareham, in common with most other towns and cities in the United Kingdom, celebrated the peace with a spontaneous outbreak of street parties. When the war ended in 1945, so in a way did the old pre-war Fareham. Big changes were on the way for both the town and its people.

CHAPTER NINE
Prest à Faire

The end of the war brought hopes of a better future for the weary, battered people throughout the country. In Fareham, those hopes were amplified by the desire of many visionary people to achieve for the town the prestige and dignity of borough status. This had first been mooted during the late 1930s — a decade in which Fareham's population had almost doubled from 20,000 to 40,000. The war had delayed the Urban District Council's application for borough status, but local councillors were soon busy putting together the statistics and organizing their new plan of campaign. On 10 December 1946, the petition for a "Charter Incorporating the Inhabitants and Urban District a Municipal Borough" with Fareham's badge — including its Prest à Faire (Ready to Do) legend — proudly adorning the title page was presented to "the King's Most Excellent Majesty in Council". This petition, besides listing the town's advantages and supplying the data to back its claim, emphasized that a charter of incorporation would encourage the more efficient performance of public duties and would also be "a tribute to the loyalty, steadfastness and worth of the inhabitants when the threat of invasion was very real."

The petition stressed that the town had cooperated fully with the armed services throughout the war and had shown efficiency and foresight in organizing shelter, first-aid facilities and fire-fighting services during the air-raids. Repairs both to houses damaged by bombs and to roads battered by frequent heavy tank traffic were well under way, the petition reported. And, throwing moderation to the winds, the Urban District Council claimed: "Had atomic energy been first discovered by our enemies and destroyed the towns of this country

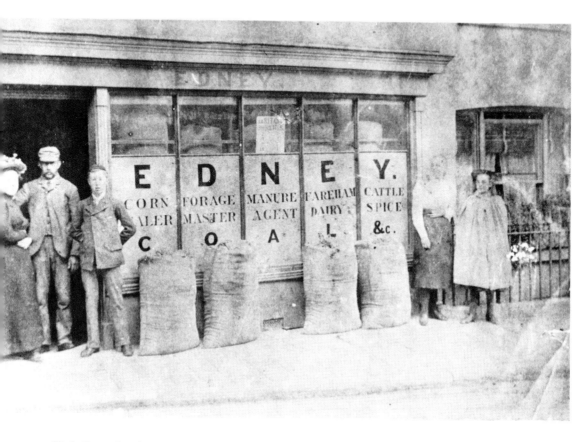

*High Street Fareham 1879. The Edney family operated Fareham's
Chesapeake Mill at Wickham and ran this shop at the southern end of the
High Street. In addition to the staples advertised on the front of the shop
they also sold, according to the small hand-bill, Sanitary Briquettes!*
Photo by kind permission of B. Tappenden.

the foundation stone of the new England would have been most certainly in precisely the position occupied by Fareham today. Whether the planners would have chosen the position of her key towns from ideas of commerce, healthy atmosphere, surroundings, communications, or simply on the score of a symmetrical map, Fareham's geographical situation was ready-made for the purpose."

After such high hopes, so powerfully expressed, the ultimate refusal by the Privy Council to accept the plea — after a delay of three years — must have been a massive disappointment to Fareham. Five years later, the Urban District Council submitted another plea for incorporation and yet again its application was turned down, with no reasons given for the refusal. Meanwhile, however, other schemes were afoot, schemes which were to have great bearing upon the change between the Fareham of the 1940s and the town we know today. In 1947, the Town and County Planning Act laid upon the nation's county councils the task of preparing twenty-year development plans in a spirit of rebuilding for the long-term future. Hampshire County Council was one of the first authorities to submit its development plan and it was generally regarded as one of the best. The County Council required Fareham among other Urban Districts to prepare a town-development map complete with suggestions for future land-use, building schemes, and roads. This long-term project was naturally constantly revised, discussed, and disputed. Controversies arose from time to time, not only between individual councillors but also between the County Council and the Urban District Council. Fareham, for example, was anxious to develop its Western Wards but was frustrated to some extent by the rather rigid Green Belt proposals of the County Council.

The constantly rising population, the alarming increase in the number of road vehicles, and the need for new housing of reasonable quality all combined to alter the situation from year to year, resulting in more plans and more amendments to plans. But it is worth noting that as early as 1957, when the Comprehensive Development Area Map for

Another photograph of the Cedar Cottage tea rooms on the corner of Bath
Lane, this time showing the rear of the premises. It served as the mess
for operational staff from the anti-aircraft defence headquarters at
Fareham House in the Second World War. Later it was incorporated into
the Cedar Garage.

the town centre was submitted to the Minister of Housing and Local Government, it contained provision for using twenty acres of land between West Street, High Street, Osborn Road, and Westbury Road for shops, a civic centre, and car parks.

Some people would have preferred Fareham to stay as it was. In the 1950s and even into the 1960s it retained its market-town character. There were plenty of interesting shops and some comfortable cafes where, it was claimed, individual service was still the norm rather than the exception. A guide book to Fareham produced in the early 1960s describes the town as "busy yet tranquil, steeped in history, rich in soil, scenery and splendour," and has this to say about the shops: "If a visitor were asked what was the main industry of Fareham, he would not be far wrong in answering 'shopping', for the shops and pavements give the impression, a correct one, that everything is provided to encourage people to enjoy their shopping expeditions." But as the affluent, consumerist society of the 1960s progressed, there were many who found this market-town image of Fareham wanting. Evidence began to grow that the rising population often preferred shopping in Portsmouth or Southampton, and that there was a tendency for visitors to regard Fareham more as a place from which to explore other and more interesting spots than as an attractive town in its own right. West Street, as far as traffic was concerned, was becoming a tangled mass on Saturdays and Mondays in particular, when the market was operating. Crossing the eastern end of West Street was hazardous, with busy traffic on both sides of the road and cars and vans parked not only on the roadside but in the middle of the street as well. Although the Urban District Council had tried to alleviate the West Street problems by providing car parks in Quay Street and Osborn Road as well as the use of the market-place, those were the days before the advent of double-yellow lines and motorists still preferred to fight for kerbside spots. On one day in 1958 it was reported that only 62 vehicles were using the free car parks in the town, which could hold 300, while the police were resignedly attempting to solve severe traffic problems caused by cars trying to park in West Street.

The top end of the High Street in the late 1930s. On the left-hand side of the street just where the small car is parked is the Elsa Tea and Dining Rooms. In the left foreground is a lorry from local builders' merchants G.A. Day.

The increase in the numbers of vehicles in Fareham with its attendant delays, dangers, and congestion, together with the increasing population, caused many furrowed brows during the 1960s. As neighbouring Gosport was also growing quickly, there was some speculation and discussion concerning the possible merger of the two towns into a single county borough. Both councils held talks about a possible amalgamation — and who knows what this area would have been like today if agreement had been made? But local pride won the day. The two towns decided to retain their individual identities, and Fareham could now concentrate upon its own destiny. A significant landmark was the appearance in December 1965 of a new town centre map drawn up by Shingler Risdon Associates under the auspices of Fareham Urban District Council. This publication, so far the most comprehensive analytical survey of the town and its environs, described Fareham's contemporary state very thoroughly and made major proposals for shopping, land use, and traffic to be implemented by the mid-1980s. At that time many of the proposals seemed revolutionary, delighting some local residents and horrifying others.

The town centre map gives an interesting description of the Fareham of a quarter of a century ago: "There is little recognised pattern to existing shopping other than a marked lineal one along both north and south sides of West Street, generally having no depth of development beyond the single shop premises....this ribbon type commercial development has produced an uneconomic sterilization of valuable backland," wrote the authors, concluding that the Fareham of 1965 did not offer the variety of retained choice that its catchment population required. The report urged that development in depth should take place from Quay Street to Westbury Road north of West Street, within which should be provided a new shopping complex "in the form of a precinct linked to proposed new car parks and civic buildings", together with the provision for more shopping between Quay Street and Hartlands Road south of the main thoroughfare. As for the traffic problems, a contemporary traffic census discovered that about 40,000 vehicles a day entered the central area, half of which were

High Street in the mid-1930s. On the right is T & J Edney again and next door to them is Maison Marianne & Dormie, Ladies' High Class Hair Dresser and Beauty Salon. On the opposite side of the road is Cooper the tobacconist.

actually passing through Fareham on their way elsewhere. To alleviate the growing problem, the report suggested the provision of two dual carriageways parallel to the town centre for the through traffic, with a link to the planned south-coast motorway. Among the consultants' many conclusions was the far-sighted comment that the increased shopping demand might well be merely "a token of the real potential if the regional planning of the area, with Fareham as the nodal point, takes the shape and pattern that is already emerging".

Thus the stage was set for the vast changes that were to alter Fareham so much within a few years. Before work could begin on these major changes, the plans went through various stages with modifications and new recommendations, and eventually in 1971 Hampshire County Council granted outline permission for the first phase of the shopping-area scheme. From that date onwards, it may be safely said that for over a decade the dust never settled in Fareham as demolition men and construction workers moved in. By 1982 Fareham was totally transformed. It possessed not only a large shopping precinct but also civic offices, a swimming pool in Park Lane, the Ferneham Hall, and a new football and sports area at Cams Alders, as well as the dual-carriageway road parallel to the railway line. In addition, almost quietly by comparison with the furious building activities, but just as important for the town's prestige, Fareham had at last achieved borough status in 1974. By this time, the brand new library had been completed with facilities to match the town's new dignity. For over twenty years, Fareham's library service had been housed in a rather grim building known as the Flying Angel which had been originally opened as a temporary mission for seamen during the Second World War. The large and luxurious building that replaced it in July 1973 presented a magnificent contrast. The new library, built upon a site barely 100 yards from its predecessor, cost £300,000 and was opened by Lord Portchester who wished "every possible enjoyment to the people of Fareham in this wonderful new building."

The massive development project naturally attracted

West Street Fareham in the 1930s looking east. On the left is Harold Job the jewellers and in front of the next door shop is a delivery bicycle complete with sturdy wicker basket.

much attention from the local press, with most interest and speculation concerning the shopping centre (soon to be blessed with the name Westbury). Phrases appearing in print such as "giving the town centre a new heart", "a development way above the standard of centres in the south's two main cities", and "the most important shopping centre in Hampshire outside Southampton and Portsmouth" must have been music to the ears not only of the council, but also of the architects, Siefert & Partners, and of Samuel Properties Ltd., who were responsible for the development. The clearance of the sites for the Crown offices and the shopping precinct fascinated not only casual spectators but also archaeologists — the South Hampshire Archaeological Rescue Group, working there in April 1973, unearthed some Roman remains including pottery, tiles, ironware, and parts of a ditch.

In June 1975 an article in the *Southern Evening Echo* praised Fareham as "a busy town with a bright future". Looking forward to the opening of "phase I, part I" of the new Westbury precinct, the writer exclaimed: "Not so long ago, Fareham was a rather unimpressive little town....Now it is a busy-every-day town....". After describing how the new Portsdown Hill Road had relieved the town of much unnecessary through traffic, the writer concluded, "as a result, visitors will find those old bumper-to-bonnet queues a thing of the past." But new-style Fareham was not to everybody's taste. In the uncertain economic climate of the mid-1970s, warning voices were raised about many aspects of the new development. Some claims made by the opponents of change read strangely today. The multi-storey car park was criticized not only on aesthetic grounds — not surprisingly — but also as being totally unnecessary — "nobody will use it". There was also some criticism from local motorists that the car park was the first one in Fareham that actually made a charge (5p) for its use. Meanwhile the whole development plan was derided by some who could not envisage that shopping in particular could ever develop beyond its 1970s level. There were claims that the new pedestrian precinct in West Street was diverting trade to Portchester and Titchfield and that customers wouldn't use the banks because they could not park their cars

36. EAST STREET, FAREHAM

East Street Fareham in the 1930s. One of a fine series of photographs taken by Sidney Smith of the Fareham area, some of which appeared as postcards. This one reveals a sign of times to come with the opening of The Cedar Service Station. The latter boasted, according to the sign, such new-fangled trappings as 'electric petrol pumps, car maintenance, free air and cloak rooms' among its services to passing motorists. No doubt the modest scale and restrained presence of this garage would not suit the marketing men of the 1990s.

outside any more and therefore would run the risk of being mugged. The precinct, it was even claimed, was "designed to cause chaos in the minds of shoppers". Added to these moans were dire prognostications that within a couple of years Fareham would have become a "ghost town".

Generally, however, the shoppers liked the new precinct. The summer of 1976 saw some pretty substantial "ghosts" crowding into the new air-conditioned malls, visiting the new large shops, and enjoying snacks at the green and white tables in the garden restaurant. A retired naval officer from North End was so impressed with his first visit to the new Fareham precinct that he wrote a letter full of high praise to the local press; he mentioned the ease of parking, the "cool, clean, attractive and delightful atmosphere" and concluded, "My grateful thanks to Fareham planners for providing such a service which is in such obvious contrast with that provided by Portsmouth in Commercial Road, the Tricorn and North End."

By the autumn of 1976, Marks and Spencer's store had opened to add further attraction to the shopping precinct, incidentally creating 130 new jobs. Despite all the talk of economic recession and all the gloomy predictions about multi-million-pound flops, Fareham was prospering as never before. The old phrase "shoppers' paradise" was trotted out for an airing again in the local press as the 1976 Christmas shopping period saw record takings and as many as 85,000 shoppers a week. With the new precinct an obvious commercial success, its detractors sought and found other angles from which to mount their criticisms. There were some complaints from traders outside the new centre that the council was neglecting their interests, especially considering their years of stalwart service to the town, compared with their attitude to the favoured fledglings of the precinct. One of the now-ubiquitous free newspapers publicized a line of thought called "Shop Fresh Air Fareham" which extolled the virtues of shopping outside the precinct, praised the individuality of the Fareham shops that were not branches of national multiples, and scorned some of the features of the Westbury — "...piped music, shiny

44. West Street. FAREHAM.   Photo. by — Sidney Smith.

The western end of West Street in the 1930s, looking east with a glimpse of Trinity Church spire above the rooftops. On the right is Alf Spender's fish and chip shop while the garage next door feels it neccessary to remind passing trade that Regent petrol is British! Note the handsome 'question mark' lamp standard.

floors, clean and efficient with a few green plants...". Elsewhere, fears were voiced about the ethics of giving over a
town so much to the process of selling without having provided anything more purposeful for the local community. A
letter to *The News* in May 1979 complained that Fareham "has
now irretrievably lost the individual identity of a pleasant
market town which was such a pleasing characteristic up to
only a few years ago." There were worries over what would
happen to the market if a new department store were to be
built on the site. There were suggestions that the council was
losing touch with public opinion, while the Fareham Society,
having unsuccessfully asked the Department of the Environment to preserve Church Path, put pressure upon the local
authority for a re-think and re-appraisal of Phase II of the
shopping precinct proposals in the hope that the changes
would not merely be the provision of more and more shops.

But still people came to buy in their thousands and,
as one mother with a toddler and a smaller child in a push-
chair intimated, it is more pleasant to shop in a place where
you know that your young ones are safe alongside you rather
than to battle through crowded pavements worrying about
being jostled into the path of heedless motorists fighting for
kerbside parking places. Shopping, however, was not the only
area of discussion regarding the new town centre.

Not for the first time, there were complaints from all
sides concerning the singular lack of amenities for recreation
and culture in the borough. Young people grumbled that
there was nothing to do in Fareham in the evenings except to
go out to pubs or perhaps the cinema. Older people complained that many of "their" pubs had been taken over by the
younger, rowdier element. Of course, there were those who
could see little point in wasting time and money in pubs, but
such of them who desired more aesthetic or cultural pleasures
found no outlets for their enthusiasms in Fareham (or, for that
matter, precious little in nearby Portsmouth either). People
mindful of Fareham's heritage found it hard to believe that a
town with such a large population had not even a museum.
It seemed an ironic indication of the lack of cultural facilities

THE QUAY FAREHAM

SIDNEY SMITH
PHOTOGRAPHER

Another Sidney Smith view, this time of The Quay, with a group of local youngsters posing for the camera in the foreground. A coaling coaster, the Ngandna, is unloading at the quay and into the barges alongside.

in the town that Westbury Manor, left vacant by the transfer of council offices to the new civic centre, was under consideration for conversion to a gambling casino. The Fareham Philharmonic Society, a town institution throughout the century, was reduced to performing at Portchester and they, together with other dedicated amateur groups, needed better facilities within the town. It is true that the Philharmonic Society, accompanied by the Hampshire Youth Orchestra, performed a very successful Jubilee Concert in aid of the Prince of Wales' Jubilee Charity Fund in the shopping precinct in 1977, but what was really needed, it was thought by many, was some sort of public hall.

Eventually in 1978 the council produced plans for a one-million-pound, multi-purpose public building. The scheme was promptly attacked by the local Labour Party who claimed that such a hall would be merely a prestige project irrelevant to most people in the town, advocating instead the development of more community facilities in schools and other neighbourhood centres. The new scheme, however, went ahead and, despite rising costs, due partly to the soil of the new site turning out to be full of tangled tree stumps and rusty metal, opened as the Ferneham Hall with a gala weekend in February 1982, with the star attractions including Cilla Black and Don Maclean. Despite many fears to the contrary, Ferneham Hall has housed the productions of local amateur theatre, opera, and music groups as well as those of professional entertainers. It has also served, as was intended, many other functions and its extra provision of a coffee and lunch bar has provided a welcome amenity to many shoppers. Meanwhile, to the delight of many local enthusiasts, a fine new swimming pool was built in Park Lane, later to be developed during the health-obsessed 1980s into a leisure centre with a variety of sporting facilities.

Eventually, too, Fareham got its museum. Westbury Manor, the elegant old building which had for so long stood disused and forlorn, fittingly became the home for the borough's museum. Back in 1979, a public-spirited woman, Winifred Cocks, had left her house, 26 Wickham Road, to the

A pleasant prospect of the Upper Wharf with Fred Dyke's Repair Shop & Quayside Garage. Fareham Flour Mills in the background and to the right Thomas Gater Bradfield & Co. Ltd., grain merchants.

council for use as a museum. The offer was rejected on the ground that this would put the museum too far out of town. Nonetheless, Miss Cocks's offer may have made the authorities realize how conveniently sited, near the shops, was Westbury Manor. The museum will, it is to be hoped continue to foster that sense of community that is vital if the expanding conurbation that Fareham has become is to retain a sense of identity. The displays in the museum provide the necessary historical linkage between the scattered villages, the now-departed industries, and the modern commercial complex in the town.

The establishment of the museum is, perhaps, one example of the extent to which, in the 1980s, public opinion helped shape Fareham's development. The excellent and civic-minded Fareham Society battled with developers, and sometimes with the council, to keep intact what still remained of the old market town of Fareham and its attractive green fringe of villages. While recognizing the need for inevitable changes, vigilante groups like the Fareham Society endeavoured to persuade planners and developers alike to preserve a balance between the need to provide new jobs and housing and the very real desire of local people to keep something of Fareham's market-town ethos. The result of this power struggle was an unprecedented number of appeals lodged against developers. From 1984 to 1986 there were 102 separate appeals — an average of one a week — resulting in public enquiries. This must be one of the highest appeal rates anywhere in the United Kingdom, but it does prove beyond doubt that both the council and the residents were, as they still are, well aware — to paraphrase a famous maxim — that the price of sensible planning is eternal vigilance.

The history of Fareham is a continuing thing. We have seen the little Saxon settlement transformed over the centuries into the flourishing market town depicted in some of the photographs in this book. The old Fareham industries of brickmaking, tanning, and pottery have now gone, to be replaced by a new type of industry and commerce dominated by the computer. The rich strawberry fields have largely given

Titchfield Road and Fareham railway bridge, looking west with the old toll house in the far distance.

way to the new shopping complexes. Serried ranks of parked cars occupy the fertile earth once trodden by the heavy horses with their carts laden with lush produce from the village smallholdings. But history is still being made in Fareham, as it goes forward "ready", as its motto assures us, "to do".

The Borough crest   *By kind permission of Fareham Borough Council*

*Aeriel view of Fareham in the 1940s. The Creek is tranquil, Gosport
Road has little traffic and Elmhurst Road and Belvoir Close are shining in
the sunlight. A steam train hurries towards the viaduct on the
Portsmouth line. The buildings on the north side of West Street present a
variety of frontages, the most prominent being the 1930s Savoy Cinema.
At this time Fareham could still claim to be a 'small market town'.*

Aerial view of Fareham in the late-1980s. Eastern and Western Ways together with the railway line act as a boundary to contain the bustling town centre. On the left Wallington Way takes Portsmouth-bound traffic away from the High Street whilst Park Lane, Harrison Road with the Junior School and the Old Turnpike and Serpentine Road are prominent in the foreground. In the distance, Fareham Lake leads out to the sea between Portsea Island and the Gosport peninsular.

ACKNOWLEDGEMENTS

The authors would like to record their appreciation to the many people who helped in differing ways in the preparation of this book. Their thanks go to the staffs of the Fareham, Portsmouth, and Gosport libraries; to David Nye, Assistant Director of Planning, Fareham Borough Council; to Brenda Clapperton of the Fareham Society; to Alice James of the Fareham Local History Society; to Charles Bass for the loan of a family document; to Margaret Bell, Joy Dingle, Margaret Cawte, Herbert Rea, and Chris Webb for their personal reminiscences; to Keith Dingle for his expert photographic work; and, lastly, to Alastair Penfold, who allowed us free access to the Fareham Museum document and photographic collection at a time of great upheaval for him and his staff while Westbury Manor was being converted to museum use.

BIBLIOGRAPHY
And Further Reading

Brown, Ron. *The Fareham of Yesteryear*. Ensign Publications, Southampton 1983.

Burton, Lesley. *D-Day: Our Great Enterprise.* Gosport Society Publications, 1984. *Gosport Goes to War*. Gosport Society Publications, 1981. *The Life and Times of Gosport Grammar School*. Lesley Burton, Gosport 1989.

Cobbett, William. *Rural Rides* (edited and with introduction by George Woodcock). Penguin Books, London 1967.

Cunliffe, Barry. "The Saxon Culture at Portchester Castle" in *Antiquaries Journal*, Vol. L, part 1, 1970.

Fareham County Primary School. *In the Beginning: the Early Years of Fareham County Primary School*, Fareham [nd].

Glasspool, John. *Solent Shores*. Nautical Books, London 1988.

Glenn, David Fereday. *One Hundred Years of Roads & Rails around the Solent*. Ensign Publications, Southampton 1991.

Hampshire County Council. *Outline Plan for the Portsmouth District, 1949-1963: (Final Report by the Max Lock Planning Group)*. Hampshire County Council, Winchester 1949.

Horn, Pamela. *Labouring Life in the Victorian Countryside.* Allan Sutton, Stroud 1987.

Hughes, Michael. *The Small Towns of Hampshire*. Hampshire County Council, 1983.

James, Alice (ed.) *Fareham Past and Present* (booklets). Fareham 1965-

Knight, R.J.B. (compiler).*The American War: a Calendar* (Portsmouth Record Series. Portsmouth Dockyard Papers, 1774-1783). City of Portsmouth, 1987.

Minns, Rev. G.W. "On a Portrait of Lady Betty Delmé, by Sir Joshua Reynolds, formerly at Cams Hall" in Proceedings of the Hampshire Field Club, Vol.III, 1895.

Mitchell, V., and Smith, K. *Branch Lines to Alton.* Middleton Press, Midhurst 1984 and *Portsmouth to Southampton.* Middleton Press, Midhurst 1986.

Moore, Pamela. *Bygone Fareham.* Phillimore, Chichester 1990.

Morris, Christopher (ed.). *The Illustrated Journeys of Celia Fiennes,1682-1712.* Macdonald/Webb & Bower, Exeter 1984.

Pevsner, Niklaus, and Lloyd, David. *The Buildings of England: Hampshire and the Isle of Wight.* Penguin Books, London 1967.

Privett, George. *The Story of Fareham.* Warren & Son, 1949.

Robertson, Kevin. *The Railways of Gosport.* A. & C. Black, London 1988.

Simmonds, Roger and Robertson, Kevin. *The Bishops Waltham Branch Line.* Wild Swan Publications, 1988.

Stapleton, Barry, and Thomas, James H. (eds.) *The Portsmouth Region.* Alan Sutton, Stroud 1989.

Watts, George (ed.) *Titchfield: a History.* Titchfield History Society, Titchfield 1982 and Watts, George & Wade, Richard (eds.) *Titchfield: a Place in History.* Ensign Publications, Southampton 1989.

White, Leonard. *The Story of Gosport* (new revised edition by Lesley Burton and Brian Musselwhite). Ensign Publications, Southampton 1989.

Wood, Stevens, Rev., and Capes, Rev. W. "The Bishops of Winchester" in *Winchester Diocesan Chronicle*, 1907.

Victoria County History of Hampshire. Vol. 3, 1908 (reprinted 1973).

Documents, reports, and local plans prepared by the Fareham Urban District Council, Fareham Borough Council, and Hampshire County Council, 1946-1991.

The Hampshire Structure Plan, Winchester 1972

Fareham town directories, 1800-

Hampshire Magazine, Southampton.

The News, Portsmouth.

The Southern Evening Echo, Southampton.

Fareham Town Centre Plan reproduced by kind permission of Renton Howard Wood Levin Partnership

EXIST

PORTLAND
CHAMBERS

Public
House

WESTBURY MANOR

office
entrance

market traders store

WESTBURY MANOR
GARDENS

Flat

escalators

SHOPS

Flats

SHOPPING M

SHOPS

BUS STATION

HARTLANDS ROAD

Toilets
Bus
Station
Office

spira
to c

FAREHAM TOWN CENTRE
GROUND FLOOR PLAN

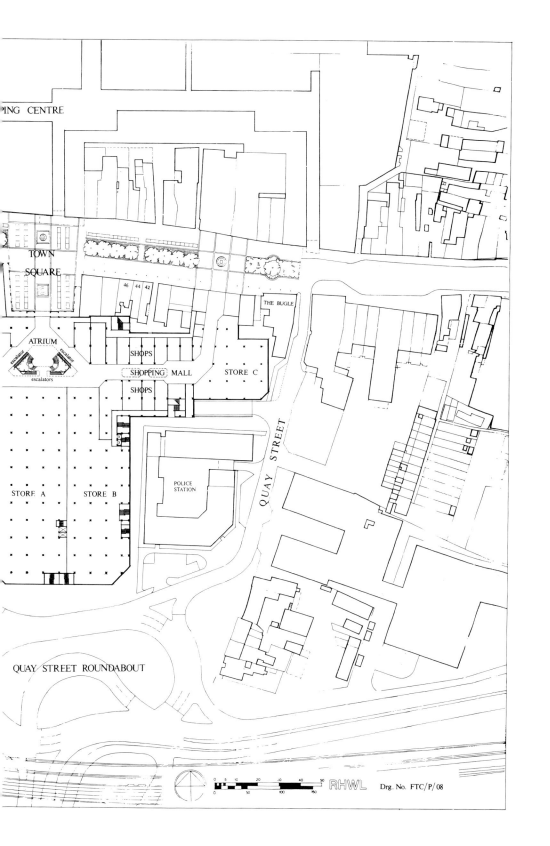

INDEX